They're Coming for Your Elders
and
Your Inheritance

They're Coming for Your Elders
and
Your Inheritance

Ways to Protect Your Family, Mitigate the Damage, and Change the System

Léonie Rosenstiel

Published by Dayspring Resources Inc.

ISBN (paperback): 978-1-962888-02-8

ISBN (ebook): 978-1-962888-03-5

Book design and production by www.AuthorSuccess.com

ILLUSTRATION CREDITS: Judy Peterson and Freepik (Chapter IV), Pixsbay (Chapter VI), ID 216047479 © Pikepicture | Dreamstime.com (Chapter VII)

Printed in the United States of America

To Steve Harrison, Laura Harison, Patty Aubrey and, most of all to Jack Canfield, who made me realize that solutions, even to major problems, lie all around you. Knowing where to look and which questions to ask can be the keys to solving the hardest puzzles.

And to all families whose members are not saints.

DISCLAIMER

The information in this book is not intended as legal or medical advice, nor is it intended to provide specific guidance for anyone's individual situation. It is intended as education—to make your planning easier. It provides a larger perspective on what's happening, why it's happening, how you might be able to discover the best possible outcomes (while avoiding those that might harm you and your family), and what you and your loved ones most need.

For a free and quick check on whether you understand what's involved financially in caring for a dependent adult, please see the download, available at:

https://dayspringresources.com/7-ways-to-get-financially-empowered/

Contents

Foreword

When I read the first book Léonie Rosenstiel sent me, I called my attorney to ask whether the sorts of legal horrors she described could possibly happen. "They happen all the time," he assured me.

Léonie had written a memoir about how she, her husband, and her mother, who was suffering from dementia, had been treated during Leonie's difficult fourteen-year odyssey through the court system in search of justice and equity.[1] I was appalled.

Then, I wrote the foreword for her next book, an attempt to make sure people who are neither extremely wealthy nor extremely poor have access to affordable legal services. Some people call this "the New Law," since it tries to level the legal playing field a bit.[2]

They're Coming for Your Elders and Your Inheritance is the third book she's written that I think it's important for people to read. Here, she turns her attention to critiquing the whole system of elder care, dementia, and family dynamics, but with compassion for everyone involved. If there's a benign explanation for the way people are acting, she'll always give them the benefit of the doubt. However, sometimes what happens is just plain wrong. Most people who read these stories will come to the same conclusion.

As a trained and expert researcher, Léonie writes with authority about real people and real situations. You don't want to experience events like these in your own life, so Léonie does whatever she can to give you methods for avoiding the worst-case scenarios.

Léonie is a cultural whistleblower. She has a deep knowledge of the legal system and how it affects families, and she has a passion for making things right. She knows, in detail, what's wrong, because she has lived through some of the worst aspects of it herself and observed similar things happening to hundreds of other families. But she also has some good ideas about how people with the right motivation and goodwill can fix the problems in our legal system—and particularly those relating to elders and their families—that many of us struggle with daily.

By suggesting methods of gaining financial freedom for yourself, she can also help to map out strategies to empower you to make decisions, when needed, based on what's best for your family and not just for your current budget.

You need to learn what Léonie can teach you. It will save you a world of grief (and perhaps a lot of money, too). It will help your family stay together through adversity. If your family members are not together in spirit now, it will help them come together for the greater good of every member of the group. Because, as she shows in this book, the alternative is chaos and pain, a fractured family, and sometimes even financial hardship that may last for the rest of your life.

I'm not a big fan of motivating people by fear, but in this case, learning about what can happen to you and your family if you don't fully understand the realities of what you are about to read justifies a jarring wakeup call. This book is that call . . . from someone who deeply cares for you.

—Jack Canfield, Coauthor of the Chicken Soup for the Soul® series and The Success Principles™; How to Get from Where You Are to Where You Want to Be

Introduction

Even though *They're Coming for Your Elders and Your Inheritance* is about our seriously flawed elder care and guardianship system, it is a book of hope. Hope forged in the crucible of pain and fear. Hope, with its difficult birth, techniques, and processes is explained so that readers will not have to experience the same problems and live out the same dramas I describe.

This doesn't apply to me, you might think. *My elder loved ones are all healthy. There's lots of paperwork, but it's all in order.* This book will show you how easily our current legal system can prove this belief mistaken.

What might happen to you if you don't read this book? Well, how much money, time, health, and peace of mind do you stand to lose? Might you end up like one of the families whose stories I'm about to tell you, or the others whose tales you'll hear about later in this book, the ones who learned too late?

In 2012, John Pittas of Pennsylvania didn't think it was fair that a judge ordered him to pay his mother's $93,000 nursing home bill. She had already moved to Greece to be with his two sisters, and no one had sued his mother or his sisters. John kept lawyers busy filing two appeals. After he lost them both, he had to pay not only his mother's bills but his own legal fees, as well.[3] As of this writing, twenty-six states allow these sorts of claims.[4]

Elden and Rita Lindercamp had a similar experience about a year later. The North Dakota nursing home to which Elden's elderly parents had owed a total of $104,000 sued Elden *and his wife* to collect that money. North Dakota's Supreme Court denied his appeal. The nursing home won. Why? Elden had bought real estate from his parents at what the judge decided was less than fair market value shortly before they entered the facility.[5]

Spouses, parents, children, siblings, grandparents, and grandchildren are sometimes also liable. And it's about where the person who owes this money lives, not necessarily where you live. When the money one couple had dedicated to the care of their adult developmentally disabled child ran out, the court in their state required them to pay more than $200,000 to an institution in another state where he lived. A judge had decided that they had the money to pay that amount, and allowed this entity to sue them, even across state lines.

Barely two years after the Pittas case was resolved, another Pennsylvania dispute involved Joseph Eori, who sued his brother and sister. Joseph had been supporting their mother, who was then gravely ill. He told the judge that his siblings ought to be helping their mother out financially. The court ordered his siblings to pay $400 a month each toward their mother's expenses. His sister agreed to pay. His brother appealed but lost. Joseph won the court fight, but it's likely that the legal wrangling did little for family harmony.[6]

Later in this book, I'll discuss how similar problems might be avoided.

Some people regard such laws as archaic. Two states have repealed similar statutes. But consider this: increasing numbers of elders need long-term services. Care facilities are having trouble hiring adequate staff and keeping pace with inflation. At the same time, bankruptcies of senior care institutions are skyrocketing.[7] Since 2020, a record 579 nursing homes have filed for bankruptcy.[8]

A major multi-state nursing home company now has only one facility left in Florida after declaring bankruptcy. The states can't control inflation. But if they want to see that care stays accessible, they're going to have to find a way to see that nursing home bills are paid. As of 2023, the journal *Home Healthcare* claimed that bankruptcies had not seriously impacted that industry . . . "yet."[9] Which people are they likely to turn to first for payment? What do you think?

Regardless of the shifting finances of the elder care industry, you are impacted now and will continue to be as you worry about your elders. Even if a financial legacy isn't a part of the picture, there's a lot more involved. First, your peace of mind goes. If you become a caregiver, you might have to deal with the loss of your own job or significant other. You might find yourself unable to sleep well at night, perhaps for years on end. That situation, in turn, will endanger your own health. At the very least, it can weaken your immune system.

"I was blindsided when my father developed dementia!" my friend said.

He had told this to many people. We all wondered why that diagnosis had come as such a shock to him, because his mother had died three years earlier from the same cause. Her diagnosis, and its aftermath, might have been a wake-up call, at least inducing him to prepare for a few 'what if' scenarios.

He didn't do that. Instead, he ended up trying to manage his own serious depression and his father's decline simultaneously, and without help, as if he were dealing with an entirely new experience. Distracted, he became less attentive to his work. His decreased productivity led him to lose out on a promotion he badly wanted, which only increased his depression.

Just imagine how much worse the situation would have been if he'd been an entrepreneur! Might he have lost his entire business in the process? Distracted entrepreneurs tend to make bad decisions, both in business and in life. And what about the women, who are often stereotyped as caregivers? Women entrepreneurs, who think they are obligated to have unlimited energy, sometimes try to add caregiving to other duties, effectively working hundred-hour weeks. Eventually, burnout is almost assured.

Over the years, I've had friends who have suffered financially because of the time they spent in court. Or they stood by, seemingly helpless, as caring for incapacitated loved ones stripped them of their savings. Others took a succession of go-nowhere jobs to be ready, at a moment's notice, to return to court and fight for their loved one's comfort. Everyone I spoke to used words like "blindsided" or "shocked." "I felt under attack," was another common refrain. The moment before it happened, such an experience seemed inconceivable to them. But happen it did.

I was one of those who had trouble believing what was happening, even while I was experiencing it. But, as I awoke to reality, I managed to learn ways of coping, and ultimately techniques to avoid some of the worst aspects of the problem. And fortunately, I also learned ways of producing income without always having to work in an office daily.

When you have finished reading *They're Coming for Your Elders*, you'll have a blueprint that will both help you to prevent catastrophic losses and to prevail over them.

If there's a tiny voice inside you whispering that all's not quite well with your elders, please listen now! Many deny reality vigorously, causing themselves additional stress, which may leave them prey to illness. I've seen friends diagnosed with cancer or other serious diseases while enduring years of emotional turmoil as they work to care for one or more elders. Some of them want to believe that they're capable of working thirty-six-hour days. They're wrong.

It doesn't matter whether you're twenty-one, or thirty, or sixty, or even older. If you have elders in your circle of loved ones, you're going to need both information and techniques for dealing with predictable hazards.

You are now reading the book that I needed, but that no one had written for me to read before my troubles started. May it help you and yours to avoid or mitigate the problems that lie in wait for you!

CHAPTER I

Starting on the Journey—An Overview

S omeday, perhaps soon, you may find yourself living a life you no longer recognize. It might happen with little warning to you, just as it happened to me. I'm inviting you to enter my story now so you can experience it with me. It felt as if I was being woven into a giant spider web, from which there seemed to be no escape.

I had been living comfortably with my husband in a New Mexico home we both loved. My widowed mother had a house nearby. Everything seemed fine, until the monster attacked.

For fourteen years after that, I endured what seemed to me like a nightmare in the form of a slow-motion horror movie. Although I experienced all the fear, disbelief, and anger directly, I was also watching the events as a spectator. Since I was a writer, I automatically looked for clues and patterns. I could admire the brilliantly written script, even though I had no choice but to fight constantly against it playing out as its writers intended.

What a production it was! Slick and practiced. The cast must have rehearsed their parts innumerable times, because they performed their roles flawlessly.

As I said, it felt as if I was stuck in the enormous web of a huge, venomous spider. From my perspective, the creature was big enough to swallow a horse. Its web could have spanned a six-lane highway and reached from the exit near me on I-25 to the next one further north! So it seemed to me the creature lassoed my feet and dragged me in. Then it started immobilizing me, wrapping me in its silk, thrown over me from a distance, preventing me from fighting back or getting out.

It waved a few of its legs at me periodically, occasionally approaching me from the other side of the web, a smirk of superiority twisting its mouth, seeming to threaten to come in for the kill. Every so often, I saw other victims in the web, far away, also wrapped in silk. The spider silk coating them gleamed in the early morning sun. They didn't stay long. One morning soon after that, I'd wake from a fitful sleep to see a little blood on the web. That specific 'guest' was gone, which only froze me further in fear.

All that time, I saw the 'extras' streaming past the net. We were in a public place! Why didn't they see me? Why didn't they seem to see or hear the other captives? Occasionally, the creature would lasso a passerby with its silk and haul the victim into the net. Those nearby acted as if nothing was happening, even those directly in front of or behind the new victim. They went on about their lives, oblivious to the danger all around them.

Although I lived in terror of the spider, each time it directly threatened me, I discovered that it had designed its threats primarily to frighten me. But then, I told myself, the other victims had been real. I'd seen them, then they were gone. One of these times, I knew that I would be the creature's dinner myself. Every day, I was grateful to have been spared. The process remained distracting, to say the least. Each time I freed any part of my body, the spider would coat me in more and more silk, so it became harder and harder to move.

Eventually, I was both a hostage and afraid to leave. Why? The spider had caught both Mama and me at about the same time. Mama wasn't far away. I wanted to free her, but I couldn't. The more I fought, the tighter the spider wrapped both of us. It threw us morsels of hope periodically, but real hope was only a mirage during those years. Along the way, I figured out how to save my husband from becoming the spider's prey and joining us in the web.

"Someone has to tell the story," Mama managed to say through her spider silk. "It can't be me anymore. You have to do it!"

Although I promised her that I'd warn others, I was still a prisoner myself.

Suddenly, I made out the silhouette of a knight-errant in full armor on his steed. Miraculously, he was able to see us. He'd been watching from a distance. Mama had just died, still a prisoner. The spider was busy patching the other end of the web as the knight approached.

"I can cut one of you free. Which should I take? I'll come back for the other one, with reinforcements."

"Take Mama! She needs attention first."

The spider didn't seem to hear us. After the knight carried Mama off, the spider noticed the hole in the web. Angry, the creature threw a thick coating of silk over my mouth, gagging me to prevent me from warning others. Then the spider patched Mama's area of the web, but suddenly lost interest in me, seemingly distracted by a temporary desire to entrap other potential victims. I guessed that the creature figured I wasn't going anywhere, so it could haul in a few more 'guests' before punishing me.

When my knight-errant came back with his retinue, they were followed by a posse of time-traveling journalists. Working together, they managed to destroy the web, but the creature escaped, perhaps to weave a new web to entrap others, who were still walking around oblivious to their own peril.

The story I've just told is only a bare outline of the saga of my mother's nine-year commercial guardianship and its five-year aftermath.

That experience converted me into a fighter for guardianship reform. The spider represents the entire legal guardianship system in those instances when it goes seriously awry. I'm talking about evildoers in the courts, among the 'elder experts,' and in the industries involved in elder care.[10]

It's strange to think there might have been any upsides to this tale. But there were, and some were huge!

Several years into this torture, seeing how my mother's drama had been playing out, as I said before, I had already learned enough to help my husband avoid the same fate. He stayed a free man until his dying day. He was my first success story. Finally, I won my own freedom and the right to share with you what I had learned, so you can help yourself. Another win, and not just for me.

As far as anyone can tell, I was the first—and remain the only—person who was totally gagged by a judge, but who legally regained full freedom of speech. Since I've gotten my freedom back, I've done my best to help others avoid or reform this system.

Using the principles outlined in this book, I hope that many more people will regain their civil rights, and others will find ways to avoid this toxic process altogether. Eventually, we'll work together to find ways to reform the process.

Over the years, I've grown able to predict many of the problems others will face.

The evil creature that captured me might secretly be stalking you too, only to drag off you and your loved ones when you least expect it. For protection, you'll need a working knowledge of the techniques and processes described in the chapters that follow.

Look at these tips as ways to save your inheritance. Look at them as ways to save your family. Look at them as ways to preserve your health. They are all of those things. They will help to keep you free. They will allow you to respond in a reasoned manner rather than react emotionally when the unthinkable happens.[11] This is a book designed to help you guard your freedom and the freedom and safety of everyone you love.

As I learned from those fourteen years of painful experience, I should have had a reservoir of knowledge about myself and my family that went far beyond simply having certain legal papers available. I also needed a wide range of information about the forces acting on me. What were they? Why were they there? What were the objectives of those who wielded them, and why did their objectives always seem to clash with what I understood to be my family's best interests? I'd never had a clue that I'd need this sort of information.

If you don't know about these forces, you don't even know what questions to ask. That means you'll be subject to manipulation. You can't make good decisions if you don't know the rules of the game.

Over the past fifty years, the United States has created an almost impenetrable thicket of laws, regulations, and bureaucracies. Each state has increasingly defined itself as entitled to intervene in what used to be called "family life." This is just as true with children as it is with elders. However, in this book, I'm going to concentrate on what happens to elders and their loved ones as a result of these laws.

Law often trumps logic. Any non-attorney who's been to court has seen how the judge gives professionals preferential treatment. If you want to tell the court something as simple and obvious as, "The sun is shining," you might find yourself required to employ an expensive scientist (an "expert") to back up your testimony.

Most of us have no idea that the confounding processes now operating exist, even when "all the family papers are in order." We need to know so we can begin to formulate plans about how we'll act in case of future need; real plans for the real world, not nice theories that will only work in an ideal world that doesn't exist.

According to the National Alliance on Mental Illness (NAMI), every year 19.86 percent of the U.S. population suffers from some sort of mental illness (including dementia). That's almost one person in five! If you do the math, that adds up to almost 50 million people.[12] Add to them the number of people who suffer from physical challenges, and that is a lot of potential prey for the spider!

The Pew Research Center tells us there's also a large number of non-institutionalized people with physical challenges. They estimate that 13 percent of people in the U.S. suffer from them, which adds up to another approximately 42.5 million people.[13]

Even if you don't know at least one of these people now, there's a very good chance that someday soon, you will. By 2050, over 16 million people who live in the United States will have a diagnosis of dementia. That's more than three times the number of people who had that same diagnosis in 2023.[14]

We hear about, and sympathize with, the families of celebrities like Tony Bennett and Casey Kasem when we read about the dissention that dementia created among their members. It's hit a long list of well-known people—ranging from Rita Hayworth and Sugar Ray Robinson to Charles Bronson and Glenn Campbell. When we get to Bruce Willis and Robin Williams, it looks like the problem is starting a bit earlier. Willis's daughter reported not being aware of the meaning of the symptoms her father had in the years before his diagnosis. Robin Williams was only sixty-three when he took his own life after suffering from the advancing symptoms of dementia.

In 2023, over 200,000 people *under the age of sixty-five* (40 percent of the total) had dementia. So, if you think dementia is only a disease of 'age,' or that only people with dementia have guardians, you're wrong. Just think of the recent cases of two adults under guardianship who were much younger—Britney Spears and Wendy Williams. No one ever claimed that Britney had dementia.

How This Might Play Out in a Family

Let's look at a family impacted by dementia. Mary, who is newly diagnosed with this problem, has two younger sisters. Henriette, the patient's daughter, is an only child. Mary hasn't seen her two younger sisters in years—by her own choice and theirs.

The youngest of the sisters—a widow—dies, leaving no children.

Jane, the surviving younger sister, unknown to Mary and Henriette, has already developed dementia. She is being looked after by Marion, the younger of her two daughters, who has power of attorney. Marion calls her aunt occasionally, but no one tells Mary or her daughter about their family situation or the dementia diagnosis.

When told about her aunt's dementia diagnosis, to cover for what has happened to her own mother, Marion insists, "No one in *our* family could possibly have dementia!"

Mary's dementia worsens. She needs a legal guardian to protect her. A niece has no rights in that state. However, the state considers siblings and children to have equal rights, even though Mary had disinherited her sisters and nieces in her will years earlier. The court contacts the patient's younger sister (or rather, speaks with Marion), mentioning that a guardianship case is in progress. Marion starts fighting the imposition of a legal guardianship, because it would prevent her aunt from changing her will to make Marion an heir.

Henriette's ignorance of her younger cousin's legal power allows manipulative individuals in the legal system to convince the court to appoint a commercial guardian. Why? Because they tell the court about dissension within the family, broadly hinting that the daughter must have done something wrong because her aunt's family seems annoyed with her. They neglect to mention the will as the cause of this contention. Their omission seems deliberate because Henriette won't even know all this has happened until years later.

Meanwhile, the court-appointed expert, who will eventually become Mary's court-appointed guardian, doesn't tell Marion that the court will never appoint her as Mary's guardian, nor will it ever change Mary's will to name her as an heir. Why not? Marion lives in another state, and the court-appointed expert wants Mary to stay where she is. Furthermore, they have already made an agreement within the professional community about who will take over when the case goes to court—and it will be neither Henriette nor Marion.

Marion keeps trying to change Mary's will, making new twice-yearly visits to Mary, up until the time when Mary breaks her hip and is immobilized. After that, the court-appointed guardian doesn't allow Mary to leave her home. Once that happens, Marion never visits again.

In the family I just described, the secrets kept harmed the family. You can read in *Protecting Mama* and its forthcoming prequels about how similar secrets changed the lives of every member of my family over the course of generations. Might the stress of keeping these secrets and the constant threat of possible exposure have been among the triggers for dementia? Might telling the truth have protected elders against the ravages of Alzheimer's? Perhaps, or perhaps not, but not feeling obligated to hide the truth would have made the elder's life—and her family members' lives—much more emotionally comfortable.

Just before major holidays, we all see articles or listen to experts who tell the media which questions to ask or information to give. They don't tell you how it might affect your life if you do. Think of how everyone wants to quiet the newly-emboldened relative who shows up on Thanksgiving and says, "Hi, Nana, have you planned your funeral yet?"

Nor do they really tell you what happens if you don't ever communicate on these issues, or if you don't ask a necessary question in the 'right way.' Without more clarification, a "yes" or "no" answer might be misleading. If you follow instructions given that way, you might create a situation for your loved one that person truly doesn't want. (I'll explain more in Chapter II about how this happens.)

If your family doesn't habitually discuss religion or money, and if you find these subjects uncomfortable, a holiday dinner might not be the best time to start. I'll discuss other options later.

Ultimately, keeping secrets destroyed my family. Dealing with the truth would have saved us so much grief! I hope to give others the gift of avoiding these experiences.

Misconceptions in These Areas Can Harm You

Here are six basic areas in which misconceptions can harm everyone:

1. Who are your friends and allies and what sort of planning can help?
2. What does "home" mean?
3. Who are the other players?
4. What about the money?
5. Publicity is always a good thing.
6. Who needs an attorney?

There's an additional question most people don't consider, going in: How long will it be before I bankrupt myself if I keep fighting the system? I'm going to talk about ways to head that problem off, as well.

What Now?

Once you know what reality is like 'out there,' you'll need a framework for deciding on your personal best course of action. What will work for your family as an ecosystem? Should you modify it now? Changing how things work today within your own family might rescue your loved ones or prevent their loss of freedom in the first place. Doing so might also protect your future health and financial wellbeing.

But change in society is hard to accomplish; it might take time. Some powerful lawyers believe that they benefit from the way things are now. Most legislators seem to be attorneys. If they're hostile to families, and their attitudes continue to control the legal system and the legislature, we'll continue to have problems. Under those conditions, the legislative and judicial branches of government are not going to enact or adopt changes that will help families flourish. (I say "adopt" because the rules the supreme court of your state adopts determine the way the courts interpret and administer the laws enacted by the state legislature.)

We have found ways to improve the quality of our lives as we age, but not to stop the clock. At least not yet. We are imperfect beings, subject to an increasing number of malfunctions the longer we live. Remember, the only way never to get older is to die young. If you don't want to do that, you probably also don't want to be taken over by the current system, with all its absurdities, abuses, and contradictions. *They're Coming for Your Elders* offers you ways to prevent that from happening.

Notes

The final section of this book contains links to sources I've used as references.

Earlier sections of this book will have shown you how much of an advantage this sort of knowledge gives you in understanding why your family works the way it does, or even why it has trouble functioning in certain ways. However, this book is an introduction to the subject; it is not a complete guide.

Conclusion

They're Coming for Your Elders contains distilled basic insights from *Protecting Mama*, as well as that book's forthcoming prequels, *Legal Protection*, my Dayspring Empowerment Course, and my Dayspring

Empowerment Summit. It will get you started on the road to more comfortable relationships with whatever is true about your family's past, with your elders, with relatives of your own generation, as well as with those who are younger. It should help you avoid entirely many of the problems I encountered and give you the tools to deal more effectively with others.

TAKEAWAYS

1. Even if you are an only child, the court may consider others to have a valid legal interest in your loved one's care.
2. It protects you to know who all the players are likely to be, and what sorts of interests the relevant court might believe that they have.
3. Knowing how manipulations are accomplished will help you to avoid them or lessen their effects.
4. If you understand the press and the legal profession, and you also understand your own goals, you are more likely to deal with the other groups in a way that best supports your goals.

CHAPTER II

Who Are Your Friends and Allies? What Sort of Planning Can Help?

If you care about people some years older than you—parents, grandparents, significant others, aunts, uncles, or friends—you'll need to know the information in this book. Even if you don't think that you need the information right now, you might find that you'll suddenly need to use it to help yourself, or someone close to you, at an entirely unpredictable time in the future. Some of the techniques you learn, you can use in other parts of your life as well.

We all prefer to believe that we'll get adequate warning, or at least that we'll have some time to plan, but so often that's not the case if we procrastinate.

No Warning

About twenty years ago, there was a large, extended family in New Mexico. All of them depended, to some extent, on the income from the family ranch. The eldest son, who lived on the property, managed it full time. His father had retired from active management a few years earlier.

The patriarch was one of those super-energetic, healthy older people with two sets of children by two different women. He had protected the family business by putting it into a trust, with the eldest son acting as trustee. The whole operation had been functioning just fine.

Doesn't that mean everything was in order and no further planning was needed?

No! One day, the patriarch was out riding and had a terrible accident. He ended up in the nearest hospital, unconscious. The hospital called his eldest son, telling him that his father had been gravely injured and was not expected to survive. It was time for the family to come to the hospital and say goodbye. The attorney who had drawn up the family trust had long since retired.

Worried, the son thought he'd better talk to an estate attorney immediately, on behalf of the whole family. He didn't know one. Neither he nor any of his siblings seemed to have needed an attorney for a long time. He looked in a phone book. There, he saw only one advertisement for an attorney who said estates and trusts were her specialty. Having a written trust should make everything easy, he reasoned.

The attorney had never met a single family member. She was a total stranger who lived in a city more than 200 miles from the family's ranch. He called her anyway. According to his later reports, the encounter started going wrong right at that first point of contact.

"I see you specialize in trusts and estates," he told her. "I need some help. Dad's in the hospital, unconscious, and not expected to survive. So, those are your specialties?"

"My legal specialties, yes. Is there a will?"

"Dad has a trust. I'm the trustee."

"Who are the beneficiaries?"

"My brothers and sisters, and our children."

"All those beneficiaries—you've got a potential emergency there. Fax me a copy of the trust and the current contact information for the beneficiaries and I'll draw up some papers. It'll take me a few hours to get to the hospital, but once you all sign those papers, you can relax."

According to her later reports, she did the son a favor, dropped everything, and rushed down to the hospital. There, she gave the son some papers to sign. He signed them immediately. The other beneficiaries, knowing he had signed her papers, agreed with whatever she asked them to do. Within a few days, the family patriarch had succumbed to his injuries.

After his father's funeral, the son discovered that the ranch was about to be sold out from under all of them. Not only would he soon have to find a new home and a new job, but also the family business was being dissolved. All the cash would be distributed to all the children, equally. There would be no further income. The documents that the attorney had asked them all to sign at the hospital were dissolution papers for the trust. The business was part of his father's trust, and the attorney had already started dissolving the trust.

Furious, and convinced that the lawyer must have done something wrong, the son complained, first to the attorney. "What did you do?" he asked her. "I called you to protect my family, and you destroyed what Dad created!"

"I only did what I was supposed to do," she answered.

Not satisfied with her answer, he told the state's Bar Association about what happened, but they also agreed with the attorney. Why? They told him that the main purpose of a trust is to have its assets distributed, as soon as practical, to its beneficiaries. And the state encourages all children to be treated equally, so no one gets "more" than anyone else. "Wasn't that exactly the situation the new attorney had just created?" the Bar Association asked the son.

Still angry, the former trustee sued the attorney. Her defense remained the same: she'd been hired (and paid) by the family trust.

All lawyers learn in law school that the purpose of a trust is to be dissolved, and that was exactly what she'd done.

In a court deposition, she argued that if the son had hired her and paid her himself, she would have given him different advice, advice that benefited him personally. However, the way things played out, she saw her legal duty as being *to the trust*, being sure that all beneficiaries got equal amounts of cash as soon as possible.

How many people who are not attorneys could even imagine this sort of situation? How likely it is that, while an adult child is distressed and coping with a parent's medical emergency, he would also have the presence of mind to ask questions that might elicit this sort of information before he signs any papers? The time to figure out the finer points of legal ethics is not during a family crisis.

The patriarch wanted his family members to receive a steady income from ranch activities. The attorney saw this as being in conflict with the trust's 'best' interest. In her mind, the only proper solution always was to have trust assets disbursed as soon as possible. Most people don't share this understanding of the various positions that the law sees as competing interests. The entire family had one set of assumptions. The law had another. Guess who won!

Even if you don't have millions of dollars, you need to know what's possible and what might get you into trouble later. Sometimes, neither law nor health policy seems logical to the public. To make matters even more confusing, laws, policies, and rules vary from state to state. Periodic legal reforms create yet another level of complexity.

Words are important. Before I tell you more, I must address the whole matter of what to call people who can no longer make complex decisions for themselves, and whom a court has found to be "mentally incompetent." Yes, I know that there's a movement afoot to change the word 'ward' to the term 'protected person.' I shy away from using 'protected person' because, after my family's experiences, and after doing years of research on this issue, I've realized exactly how painfully vulnerable these individuals are.

The way our current system operates, I think it would be dishonest to call the people who used to be called wards "protected."

What Happens to the Less Affluent?

At the other end of the economic spectrum from the family with the ranch, there's the case of a lower-middle-class New Jersey family. Their father had been a hard-working immigrant. He'd raised two children who eventually went out on their own, married, and had children, too. The father and both of his adult children had jobs and worked hard, but not one of them managed to save much.

The patriarch retired. Then his body and his mind both started to fail. First, his daughter took him in to live with her and her children. She had never realized that it was going to cost her thousands of dollars to pay for her father's needs, even if he was staying in her home. Those needs far exceeded what he received in pension and Social Security money. Eventually, she had to choose between providing for her growing children and caring for her father. Her brother then took over, eventually making the same discovery that his sister had. He would have to declare bankruptcy if his father stayed in his home much longer.

Brother and sister agreed, at that point, that the only thing they could do was to voluntarily give up their father's care to a state-appointed guardian. The first thing the newly-appointed guardian did was to sell the father's home and place him in an institution, where both his adult children and his grandchildren continued to visit regularly. The guardian took care of the paperwork for his ward's medical care and paid for the nursing home out of the proceeds from the sale of the ward's home. There was never any possibility of an inheritance for anyone. No one had ever expected any.

Then, COVID-19 struck. The facility was locked down, just like other similar institutions nationwide. Family members couldn't visit. It no longer allowed the family members to speak with their loved one on the phone, either. It upset the whole family when the institution's employees also refused to tell them anything about his condition. When they called, the institution referred them to their father's legal guardian for news.

"The guardian's the only one we can legally tell anything about your father's condition," everybody they spoke to insisted.

After that, the man's son and daughter called the guardian repeatedly, but he never returned their calls. After several months of not returning calls, the guardian called both adult children. He left voicemail messages. "Just wanted to tell you that your father died of Covid, and we buried him two weeks ago," he said.

How is it even possible that their father suffered his last illness, died, and was buried but his children were not told until much later? The law allowed this. HIPAA, to be precise. It only authorizes one person to receive medical information about the patent, either someone the patient's healthcare power of attorney says should get it or someone else required to receive it by law. If one of the adult children had also been the legal guardian, that person would have been entitled to this information, but both children had given up their legal rights to the state.

Depending on state law, a person's legal guardian is normally designated to receive all medical information. The medical personnel will then give only the guardian medical information. Theoretically, that data goes directly from a doctor or medical facility to the guardian. It is then entirely within a legal guardian's discretion whether it's shared with anyone else, and if so with whom. State law might also contain additional powers for the legal guardian in terms of notifying relatives.

Many guardians insist that they're protecting a person's privacy by not telling family members about their loved one's medical condition.

After all, if a family member wanted this information, most guardians would ask, wouldn't that person have requested to become the guardian? And wouldn't the judge have named that relative as guardian if the jurist considered them up to the job?

If a court-appointed guardian 'tells' a third person about a ward's medical condition, and there's any objection from anyone to them doing it, they might be sued for giving out any information at all, in violation of HIPAA. HIPAA penalties can be steep. They range from a minimum of $100 per infraction to a maximum of $25,000 per infraction per calendar year.

During COVID-19, all people caring for elders were besieged with questions from concerned loved ones. Was this specific guardian's silence deliberately cruel? Maybe. Maybe not. But the adult children and their progeny suffered mightily. If the guardian had given information to one of the children and not the other, might the one excluded have gotten angry and sued him? And if the guardian had been charged with two major HIPAA violations, he (his name suggests that he was a male) might have owed up to $50,000 in fines.

Is this lack of family notification unique? Not at all! A school-teacher, the mother of one adult who was disabled due to mental illness, complained to me that her son's guardian had been sent to prison for stealing state and federal entitlement money—both from her son and from more than a hundred other wards. She knew her son would need a new legal guardian because he was still unable to care for himself. She wanted to be that guardian.

At that point, the local newspaper printed an article describing a transfer to a new commercial guardian of all the convicted guardian's wards. It had already taken place. That was how she discovered that there had already been a hearing. Her son had had his new paid, state-appointed guardian appointed by a judge without his mother ever even being told that this matter was on the court calendar. She was devastated.

How 'Protective Laws' Go Wrong

A third sort of problem comes from changes in other laws, primarily those designed to 'protect' elders and to create a defensive shield, separating society from people who might harm themselves or others. These are sometimes stories of people who went to another state to visit relatives, only to find that they were placed under guardianship while there. Most often, they never regained their freedom and the courts in the state they thought they were 'visiting' never allowed them to leave.

One paid guardian separated an affluent elderly couple, then placed the husband in a dementia facility. Claiming that the wife's visits upset the husband too much, the guardian got court permission to move him to another county, where it would be almost impossible for his elderly wife to visit him. The wife might be allowed to visit, the court order said, only if she came alone, without any other family members.

"Either I drive you to the facility, or you can't visit at all," the state-appointed guardian insisted. So, the wife would be spending hours in a car with someone she already suspected was looking for things to say she had done wrong while simultaneously allowing the guardian to bill her husband for many more hours of work.

The terms under which the visits would be permitted included the requirement that the wife would be 'chaperoned' at all times by someone loyal to the guardian to make sure she only spoke about topics the guardian approved of. Afraid the guardian wanted to take her over also, the wife did not want to go anywhere with only her husband's guardian for company. Out of the spirit of self-preservation, she declined this offer of 'companionship.'

By the time the husband died several years later in a locked dementia ward with no visitors, there was almost no money to take care of his widow, despite the multi-million-dollar trust that he had paid a reputable attorney to create to protect her. In the interim, it had been administered by a nonprofit organization (approved by the court) that automatically released whatever funds the guardian requested, ostensibly for the husband's care, no questions asked.

Most People Make No Plans—and Then There Are Unexpected Expenses

Not many people have done extensive planning for retirement, just as few people have all their legal paperwork in order. Bankrate.com's May 2023 survey of workers found that 30 percent of all workers who reported having emergency savings knew they didn't have enough to cover three months of expenses.[15] Northwestern Mutual reported that Baby Boomers are doing somewhat better, but as of 2019, only 14 percent of them had savings.[16] By 2024, they reported average savings of $120,300 each.[17]

Even people who seem to have planned carefully are often not adequately prepared for medical developments. Amy Goyer, an expert in elder care who, as of this writing, is the AARP's family caregiving expert, found that she was forced into bankruptcy as a consequence of trying to care for two aging loved ones. This development shocked her and, bravely, she decided to write about her problems.[18]

If your loved one has not discussed savings or investments with you, that might be because there are none. This might also explain why your loved one might not have made a will—many people don't think it's necessary because there are few assets to bequeath.

Only 17 percent of those answering the Northwestern Mutual survey in 2019 claimed they had between $1 and $74,999 in savings for retirement. Most financial planners tell people to plan on living, in retirement, on perhaps 70 to 80 percent of their current income. Clearly, if they're making any appreciable money now, that $74,999 will disappear fast.[19] If parents have helped their offspring through school, helped with a downpayment on a house, paid for a wedding, or helped with starting a business, perhaps they've already used up what would otherwise have been their children's inheritance.

Shortly after COVID-19 hit the US, a survey by the American Advisers Group found that fully 43 percent of people over age 60 had less than $100,000 in assets.[20] Households that had higher incomes also tended to be able to save more. No kidding! You knew that already. Considering what we have all been through since then, and the progress of inflation, I'd be surprised if some of that money hadn't vanished by now.

Most financial planners used to tell people they needed a 'retirement cushion' of at least $1 million. Now, it's more like $2 million to get a 4 percent annual income of $80,000. If your loved one isn't going to watch the money run out, I suspect they'll need at least $5 million. I'll explain my reasons in Chapter IV.[21]

"But I know I can still improve. I'll even pay you privately to help me!" I heard a senior tell a physical therapist.

"No. I can only work on an MD's referral, and your time has run out. Your doctor has to follow Medicare guidelines. He won't authorize any further therapy. I'm so sorry!" I heard her reply.

Medicare offers only limited physical therapy tied to the specific problem. If your loved one improves more slowly after a medical episode or an accident than Medicare criteria specify, rehabilitation services will be discontinued before full function is restored. Then, you'll have to modify your plan to accommodate whatever degree of mobility your loved one has achieved.

Let's suppose that you want to care for your loved one. Medicare might pay a family caregiver, but only under certain circumstances, under a doctor's supervision, or with a formal plan of care. The doctor must certify that your loved one needs certain services and/or is homebound. This certification must be renewed periodically, if you can renew at all. So, it's not just a question of getting your loved one's approval and making sure your siblings or other potential heirs don't object. The state's (or federal government's) approval might ultimately determine whether you get that authorization. Insurance has its own criteria.

The expenses of attempting to care for a loved one at a distance might easily top $12,500 per year. That's not their living expense, it's what you'll be spending on travel, hotel, etc. Their expenses must also be analyzed separately.

It costs a little less to care for someone who lives nearby. Although the expense of caring for a loved one in your home might technically be lower, you'll likely be spending a lot more time with them and might not be able to work. The financial ramifications of caring for a dependent loved one can distress many people. If you'd like to cheat a bit, you can take a look at the conclusion to Chapter X, where I suggest ways to keep yourself solvent, and even make money, during this difficult time.

One commercial guardian managed to get a judge to approve annual expenditures of $249,000 for one of their wards. Who was this woman? A wheelchair-bound person in her 90s who couldn't leave her home without a rented handicapped van. She only went out to medical appointments and was living alone in a nice middle-class home, with a single health aide assisting her. Other than dementia, she had no serious chronic health concerns. She also lived in a city that didn't have the highest living expenses in the country. (According to *U.S. News and World Report*, as of May 2024, that honor went to San Diego.)[22]

After she broke her hip, the same ward's court-appointed commercial guardian took well over $600,000 out of her accounts within the following twelve months just for nurses and home health aides, with two covering each shift. This was because someone had written into the ward's record that she wanted to remain in her own home. The file mentioned no exceptions, even though she remained isolated in her bedroom for the rest of her life, complaining to visitors that the aides left her alone. She repeatedly begged to be moved somewhere with more people so she would have more company. She failed in these efforts.

Needing more than one aide per shift is the definition of someone who requires institutional care. That $600,000, adjusted for inflation, would have skyrocketed to at least $870,400 by 2024.

In other cases, commercial guardians and conservators disposed of $500,000 or more of a ward's funds in six months, often with the express permission of the court. Generally, dementia was the only known major diagnosis. The cost of all health-related services is high now. We also know that it will only rise further with time.

That's a lot of money going out. Expenses will continue to run almost 50 percent higher in larger cities like New York City or Los Angeles.[23]

Why do many elders seem impoverished? Most financial planners used to teach that it would take nineteen years for a single individual to exhaust a million-dollar nest egg if everything went according to the common 4 percent withdrawal-per-year hypothetical plan. This is an average. In my experience, people rarely conform to the average. Calculating on that basis, you can expect that a person who retires at age sixty-five and conforms to the average will run out of nest egg money completely at age eighty-four. But people are living longer and longer.[24] With a current 'full' retirement age of sixty-six, they'll be about eighty-five when the money runs out.

Yahoo Finance reported in March 2024 that only 10 percent of US seniors had $1,000,000 or more in savings.[25]

Planning takes on a whole new meaning in this context. Should you choose to accept the assignment of helping your elders, you'll be working to conserve as many assets as possible for as long as possible. You'll be trying to see that the money doesn't run out while they're still alive.

And if you're the responsible party and don't conserve assets, the state can accuse you of deliberately spending down your loved one's assets to qualify for Medicaid. As I've already shown you, many states have additional statutes on the books that might require you to contribute an amount they think is fair to support your elder loved one. I'll explain a lot more about this situation when I talk directly about finances later.

If your loved one lives for a long time with dementia, expect the disease to take over their lives and personalities increasingly. They might acquire some of the characteristics of their caregivers. You might eventually feel that you're seeing an entirely different person.

Planning in the face of all these uncertainties is beyond 'difficult.' All you can do is the best you can. Next, we'll explore how to make strategic decisions that affect your loved one's care and the quality of your life as well.

Conclusion

In my opinion, balancing the needs of the whole family is not something our legal system does well during court hearings, either in the trust and estate area or when dealing with the medical and social aspects of adult guardianship. Attorneys are supposed to represent the interests of the client. You need to know which person/entity they think they are representing. If you don't have this information, you are in danger of encountering some very unwelcome surprises.

When should you learn how the court's assumptions might differ from yours? Now, so you won't be shocked later.

TAKEAWAYS

1. You must first determine what you are trying to accomplish, and exactly who needs this work done, before asking for legal help.
2. You need to learn and to weigh your options before facing an emergency.
3. The worst possible time to make decisions is when you're upset or distracted.
4. Conflicts among competing interests often cause serious trouble. It's not your personal definition that matters, it's the law's definition.

CHAPTER III

What Does 'Home' Mean?

Is 'home' a piece of physical property or an apartment? Or is it the idea of a place where you feel comfortable? It might simply be a place where you can come and go as you wish, and where you see any visitors you choose to invite whenever you please. If it's more than simply a physical place, then being kept in a specific location beyond the time when it serves its original purposes is going to harm more than help.

The court must approve a ward's travel. A legal guardian is supposed to know exactly who is with a ward and when. A legal guardian also has the right to prevent people from seeing a ward unless the court issues orders to the contrary. And that would be true whether this was a family guardian, or a court-appointed paid guardian.

For this statement about 'staying home' to make any sense at all, first you need to identify what 'home' means to you, and you also must do the same for the person about whom you've become concerned. Are these the same lists? If you're an introvert and your loved one is an extrovert, probably not. What is important in life to them? Is it church groups? Social clubs? What if restrictions on social gatherings, like the ones we experienced during COVID-19, prevent those anyway? You'll need to try to figure out what your loved one wants their life to look like.

Safety

There are too many considerations to detail them all here. Will a person's desire to remain at home ultimately endanger that individual? Maybe it has already, but you and your loved one might not be aware of trouble lurking in what used to be a comfortable place. I spoke some time ago with someone who advises clients on buying mobility aids. "What do you do if the home can't be retrofitted, and the person still wants to live there?" I asked.

"You'd be surprised how many elders live in unsafe homes! Unsafe for them, I mean." she replied. "They just don't want to leave, or no one can convince them they're in danger."

Mobility might have little to do with age. Sometimes, physical barriers change how a person decides to live. Back in 2009, a sixty-two-year-old widow, living alone, had a car accident that made it impossible for her to climb stairs. Her house had three levels. She and her husband had lived there for years, and she loved the place.

She discovered that she could theoretically retrofit the inside of the house—at a cost in 2010 of more than $40,000 to install lifts and make several other modifications (inflation would have increased that cost to almost $58,000 by 2024). However, the steep driveway and the pitch of the garage couldn't be changed. These would continue to make it unsafe for her to put out the trash or get into her car.

It looked as if she would be stuck in that house, unable to leave without help, if she decided to stay. She would have had to hire people to run errands and put out the trash. Instead, she opted to preserve her freedom. To do that, she had to move to a different home without stairs, built on a single level that already suited her new physical requirements. Might your loved one feel the same way under similar circumstances?

Perhaps your loved one has filled out a written document. Or, sometimes, someone heard them make a casual remark like, "I always want to live in the home I have now."

If they don't also say that a change in circumstances might alter their response, what that document says (or what your loved ones may have heard you say) will be considered "the desire of the person" and gain some power to control the situation.

How Whoever Has Legal Control Changes Things

A woman was in her nineties, and most of her friends had died by then. She had always loved being out in public and performing, but when she was alone, immobilized in her own home, there was no longer any long line of visitors to perform for. After she was no longer able to walk, she told her daughter, "I didn't realize my home would become a prison."

She was under the control of a commercial, court-appointed guardian whose position was that "the documents rule."

By the time she told a visiting chaplain that she wanted to move into a place where there were more people, the commercial guardian didn't allow it, citing as the authority a values document that this ward had never signed. But they said it was from their file. They had given a copy to the judge. Once it was in the court record, no one was allowed to question its validity. Making unconditional demands, such as "I want to stay in my own home," may come back to bite you later.

Have the place where your loved one is going to live—regardless of whether it's your home, their home, or somewhere else—examined by an occupational therapist. Stylish furniture from fifty years ago may be too low to the ground now. And what about stairs or steep hills? Is this home a safe place for them now? You might also want to ask whether it will still be the 'right place' for that person if their physical or mental problems worsen.

How often will the situation need to be reassessed? And remember that you know the patient better than almost anyone else. After one woman in her nineties received a prognosis of only two weeks left to live, her daughter argued with the hospice doctor.

"She has no more than two weeks to live."

"I've known Mama a long time, and she's not going anywhere for quite a while."

"You're crazy. I'm the expert."

However, that elderly woman lived on for almost four years after that conversation, long after both the doctor and the hospice he represented had been discharged because her condition was too "stable."

Maybe you can get a physical therapist to give you benchmarks so you can do your own periodic assessment. Eventually, people with dementia may forget how to turn off stoves and lamps, or how to use a lift or climb stairs, or even how to call for help. We weren't born knowing how to do these things. If we learned them many years ago, we might also forget them.[26]

Issues in Deciding on Living Arrangements

Many people who live in what are considered affluent areas find frequent full-color postcards in the mailbox inviting them to check out various independent living and elder care facilities in their area. The photos are often lovely, showing sumptuous meals, attractive rooms, and a nice all-around ambiance. Many of these establishments belong to large, national companies. They are either franchises or owned directly by the mother company.

Something to consider: matching elders (and their families) with nursing homes and other elder care facilities is a very lucrative business. You might receive a free consultation with an advisor. Although you don't pay that person directly, the business for which they work lives off the commissions paid to them by the owners/managers of the facilities themselves. The money will eventually come from what your loved one pays to live there or what you pay to the facility if you are paying your loved one's bills.

On November 2, 2022, the CEO of a service you pay to match your elder with a facility (myelder.com) complained in his blog, "Nursing facilities and other adult care homes typically pay the referral service a sizable commission for any placement—sometimes as much as $4,000. Many of these services funnel elders to the facilities they contract with without regard to the facility's quality."[27]

Be mindful of the many forms of agreements you might encounter when one of your loved ones is entering into one of these living arrangements, called CCRCs. That acronym stands for continuing care retirement community. The options and services in CCRCs vary widely, from efficiency apartments to luxury homes. The Pennsylvania Insurance Department has posted FAQs about this subject that quote entry fees ranging from a few thousand dollars to $1 million. They also include a warning not to sign over your assets to the establishment.[28] Some places do require this, and an increasing number require your elder to give them financial and/or medical powers of attorney.

The reason for advance planning should be obvious now. You don't want to make a major decision like this while you're reacting emotionally to an emergency. That doesn't give you time to explore the legal ramifications of what you or your loved one will be signing. You also need to have the time to compare your options.

"Kickbacks" are supposed to be illegal. Medicaid and Medicare providers are not allowed to receive them. However, as Elizabeth Hogue, Esq., wrote in 2015, "The temptations are many, but there is a great deal to be lost!"

She was referring only to providers of services such as case managers, social workers, and (hospital) discharge managers, advising them to take not more than insignificant gifts with an annual total of about $392 in value (just over $512 in 2024) from any providers.[29]

Deciding What's Important

As the ancient Greek philosopher Thales told the world long ago, "The most difficult thing in life is to know yourself."

Now, you'll see how the difficulty is magnified after multiple people get involved. You'll need to know both yourself and your loved one amazingly well to make good decisions. And you'll also need to realize what is your own emotional stuff and what your loved one really means. If others are part of this picture, you'll need to understand them, too.

We're always hearing that people want to stay in their own homes no matter what else happens. We're also told that it's good, especially for dementia patients, to live in a familiar place. Sometimes this might be true. The person might be so attached to the place that leaving would be far too painful. But dementia patients often can't tell the past from the present and the future.

If they fill out a values form that says, or they tell someone, that they want to stay in their home, they might be thinking about a house they lived in fifty years ago. Maybe that house isn't even standing anymore. It pays to ask for more information.

What about moving an elder with dementia to a new location? For as long as they remember that they've been transplanted, they might be upset. But what if the home where they currently live is eventually going to be dangerous to their health? Stairs might present an actual hazard. Even if they have an elevator, will they remember how to use it? Maybe there's a flight of stairs leading up to the front door, and you can't modify that area easily with a ramp. Or they like area rugs. Or they're going to slip and break a bone because they don't want to install wall-to-wall carpet or stick some decals on the bathroom floor so it's no longer a smooth, slippery surface. Or the driveway is so steep that they can't walk up or down it anymore. If they can't get out, others must get in. Trustworthy people. Who will they be?

James Lee, a Texas-based consultant on elder housing issues who eventually started his own elder community, was working on a system back in 2020 whereby elders living independently were checked on periodically. The point was to see whether their current house was still safe for them. What modifications might be needed? Had their condition changed sufficiently so they might need to consider other housing options?[30] He ended up joining two other reformers to start a continuous dementia care support program for both people living independently and those on the premises of his establishment, Bella Groves.

The best time to make lists, if you're going to do so, is when you're fully competent. Some people attach them to their living will. Now is the time to sit and make lists for yourself. If your loved one is still up to it, have him/her make out one, as well. If not, do this yourself, being as faithful as you can to what you recall as your loved one's wishes, not yours. Also write one yourself so you have it whenever it may be needed. Make a note on the document if you're the one writing it for someone else. Perhaps others close to you have needs or wishes, as well.

You might also pick someone you trust and give that person discretion in choosing where you live. Put that in writing also. Write that you give that person the choice of whether you remain in your home or not. There should also be a backup human whom you trust. A bank is not a good option to fulfill this function if you're looking for continuity. Bank officers retire or leave. If you give a bank discretion, the bank officer who ends up making these ultimate decisions might—like the attorney I discussed, the one who dissolved the family trust in Chapter I—be a total stranger.

The 'Values' Document

Most people who promote the concept of planning for possible later physical incapacity or mental incompetence want people to write out a 'values statement' as early as possible. However, any values statement written before COVID-19 most likely wouldn't even have considered the possibility of isolation. If your loved one wrote a values statement prior to August of 2020, it might be time to revisit what they wrote to see whether it needs to be changed.

If anyone tells you there's already a values document or "values history" for your loved one, make sure your loved one (not someone else) wrote it at a time when that person was fully mentally competent. Once people have diminishing mental capacity and are easily influenced, they can be manipulated into saying that almost anything is *their* will when in fact it's someone else's. If you ever see such a document, question it immediately. When was it filled out? (It should be signed and dated.) Where? Under what circumstances? Who was in the vicinity at the time?

Once such a document has been placed in a person's file at a commercial guardianship company, or in a conservator's file, or in a governmental or court file, anyone involved in caring for that person can justify a lot of decision-making based on trying to satisfy the person's desires. If the document doesn't reflect your loved one's wishes to start with, your loved one will not get what s/he wants ever again.

Your values and your loved one's values might not be identical. Is home a place of refuge for you? Is home a place to entertain visitors for your loved one? Clearly, the reasons why you want to stay in your home will be different for the two of you.[31]

Here's a partial list of why some people say they want to stay in the house or apartment they currently occupy. In some cases, the stated desire of one will directly contradict the underlying philosophy of the one that follows it. For any number of reasons, some might no longer be safe options:

1. Having solitude
2. Being able to socialize at will
3. Working in the garden/enjoying the patio (or balcony)
4. Familiar surroundings
5. Near church or social events
6. Near friends (but what if they move away or die?)
7. Easy transportation/shopping

Now you know how to evaluate the current living situation and where your loved one wants to stay. In the next chapter, I'll explain how we got into the situation we're in now, we'll explore the dementia process in more detail, and I'll give more detailed information about why so many people, even those who tried to do everything 'right,' end up broke in retirement.

Conclusion

Once again, our court system seems to do a poor job of balancing the needs of the whole family when dealing with the medical and social aspects of adult guardianship. You need to know whose wishes are really being discussed, particularly when dealing with someone who might be easily influenced. In some cases, what's being presented as the wishes of the ward is someone else either telling them what to say or writing what they think that person should want.

TAKEAWAYS

1. Assess what you think your loved one wants and weigh that against what you know that that person needs when seen objectively.
2. Physical safety is the prime consideration for most people. Government entities generally require that need to be met first.
3. Research whether the person you love really wanted what you're being told they want.
4. Learn to separate the wishes of the different people involved so you don't confuse what you want with what they always wanted. Can you safely (for them) do what they've always wanted?

CHAPTER IV

Who Are the Other Players?

You might think that family members are the only players in the story of your loved one's journey into aging. However, the control exercised by people from outside the family has changed over time. Through gradual changes to the law, their power to control the life of your elder loved one has greatly increased. Although you might think that you know the names of close relatives, and they're the only people who'll have a voice in what happens to your elders, you'd be seriously mistaken.

Our current problems have a long history. We've inherited some very old thinking, making our situation more complex along the way. Our problems started with the idea that residents of every country 'belonged' to the government. In ancient times, it used to be to the king or the emperor. We were all 'subjects' and not independent individuals. Ultimately, the government was responsible for us.

The 'logic', if there truly was any, was that being an elder without the capacity to make decisions makes a person like a child, who is similarly considered unable to sign contracts or do many other things without parental permission. When people in their lives are unable to care for them, the state takes over children. This is a concept called *parens patriae.*[32] The state is the ultimate parent, a concept that has existed since the twelfth century. Back then, it enabled monarchs and other nobles to confiscate the inheritances of their wards.

Often, children then were seen as property. Unfortunately, the laws relating to adults under guardianship also speak primarily about them as being manipulated or controlled as if they were objects, not humans. Then, too, the state may take over, even in cases where relatives are willing to do the job. The idea is that the state is the guardian, but it deputizes someone else (often a commercial entity) to do the day-to-day job. Even when relatives are deputized, the state supervises their work. (There's some question about whether government or court scrutiny is as strict with those it considers 'professionals.')

In the United States, we have grafted the notion of adults as state property on top of our nation's history and philosophy of rugged individualism. Is it any wonder that we keep running into contradictions everywhere we look?

Your brain is designed to look for coherent patterns.[33] What you've just read likely doesn't align with your values. Internally, the guardianship system often contradicts itself. This situation upsets and disorients us. Feeling off balance leaves us vulnerable to people who are less than scrupulous and want to manipulate us for their own benefit. Sometimes, it's not all that easy for you to figure out a person's place in the system and how what they do can help or harm your cause.

In this chapter, I'll show you how what we now call guardianship and conservatorship came to be. I'll let you see how realizing there's a problem often comes long after trouble has already started to develop.

This is greatly complicated by the manipulations of professions that benefit financially by taking care of dependent people. Some of them want to complicate the process further in ways that may line their pockets with even more money while harming the public. As I've already said, they also want to insulate themselves against all complaints.

Preventing Immediate Hazards

Guardianship, as an institution, goes back to the time before the Bible. The Romans developed categories and complex rules for the sorts of decision-making a guardian could do under specific circumstances. The basic idea behind this system was that the ward was going to be a child who aged into adulthood and ultimately could make independent decisions. It was a complex system, however, and made a separate provision for 'lunatics,' a word we would now find offensive, but a least it acknowledged that they were in another category, which our current law doesn't.[34]

With dementia, the situation is not exactly the opposite, because even though a person's mental processes deteriorate, usually they have deteriorated quite a bit long before anyone takes any action to protect these individuals against themselves. Often, they have already made questionable decisions before anyone will admit they have a problem.

Some people see a dark design in our current adult guardianship system. But you don't need to believe this. Just understand that our system descends from the one that was designed to help little Roman orphans grow up and now we're trying to use it for aging modern adults with all sorts of deep family ties that commercial guardians may routinely ignore or destroy. No wonder we're having terrible problems! The system itself, as applied by insensitive individuals who happen to be some of our commercial guardians and judges, violates our social norms.

For convenience, I'm going to use female pronouns and the name "Mama" most of the time. Women generally live longer than men. But the person I'm describing might just as easily be a male as a female. By the time people reach the age of eighty, half of them will have at least some signs of dementia.

The National Institutes of Health now says most people start to show signs of dementia at about age sixty to sixty-five.[35] Mental health organizations often provide lists of signs that should raise red flags. However, none of these individual signs, by themselves, are normally sufficient. They must be seen in context.

Experts disagree about how long a person may show brain evidence of a plaque buildup in the brain before dementia symptoms show. Some say a decade, and others think it's as long as twenty years. Still others deny that plaque is the marker for this disease at all, because some people who have visible plaque in their brain never show any symptoms.[36]

Might there be ways to confirm the presence of dementia before the symptoms cause harm to the victim? Perhaps PET scans or other recently invented tests can provide a more scientific way of identifying and 'staging' (determining the extent of) the disease.[37] However, if tests are created, might they identify as potential victims people who will never develop the full-blown disease? Here are a few warning signals:

Almost everyone has missed paying a bill at some time. Perhaps even more than once. Maybe they just plain forgot because they were distracted by other matters, or the envelope slipped under a pile of papers and they didn't see the bill again until after the due date. With the increasing use of email to send invoices and the advent of automatic billing for things like mortgage payments and utility bills, I suspect this symptom will eventually not be used as much to indicate advancing dementia. But you'll still need to wonder about overdrawing a bank account.

The next classical sign of Alzheimer's will only tell you anything if your loved one used to be good with numbers but now she's having trouble following a recipe she's been using for years or is no longer paying the bills at all. If it's a new problem, it needs to be investigated. If it's been a feature of your loved one's life forever, there's a good chance that you already know that this is not a sign of some new problem.

Disorientation is another tipoff. One woman called her son, distraught. "I've been living in this town for fifty years," she complained, "then, this afternoon, I couldn't figure out how to get home from the mall!"

If navigating around a familiar town has become difficult, this is likely a sign of memory problems that need attention. Unless, that is, your loved one is in a severe state of emotional upset, like the distraction caused by the death of a friend or family member. Or maybe new glasses are on the agenda. You always need to rule out physical problems, some dietary imbalance, or a recent emotional upset before concluding that dementia has set in.

At his competency hearing, one man treated some disagreements he'd had with his daughter as a teenager as if they'd occurred recently. He told the court he was concerned about her wanting to take revenge on him for them, describing these events as if they'd only happened yesterday and she hadn't forgiven him for them. In fact, they had reconciled years earlier. He simply didn't remember that part of the story while he was talking to the judge. What happened? The court didn't allow the daughter to testify, and someone else became the man's legal guardian.

Different states have different rules for stopping older people from driving. If a new pattern of repeated accidents has become a problem for your loved one, and dementia turns out to be the cause, check on the driving laws of the state where they live as soon as possible. Surrendering a license sooner rather than later might save Mama's life, or perhaps the life of a total stranger. The Department of Motor Vehicles in your loved one's state can tell you where to look for the relevant local laws and regulations.

You need to know before you report any cognitive problems that another person might seem to have that it might kick off an inquiry into the competency of your loved one to live independently and to make decisions. If they're disoriented, is it still safe for them to travel alone, even on public transport?

An otherwise inexplicable new tendency to fall is a potentially dangerous early sign of dementia. Falls can lead to broken bones and immobility. They can also lead to concussions and further loss of mental function. Loss of balance might also signal that the blood supply to the brain is not flowing smoothly. A trip to the doctor and some tests should determine the cause of the balance problem.

So many different symptoms can give us a clue that something's not right! They range from a new habit of using the wrong word in sentences to not being able to follow a conversation.

Dementia patients might have outsized reactions to surprises, or to anything that makes them even slightly uncomfortable. They might cry or yell. They might be volatile or fearful, or exhibit some emotion that they normally didn't have before. Or their emotions might now be so exaggerated as to be inappropriate. Again, it's the deviation from the person's own normal that's important.

One mild symptom, by itself, rarely makes anyone snap to attention and worry about Mama having dementia. However, if you suddenly start finding car keys in the freezer or detergent in the refrigerator, do start worrying immediately.

Encourage Mama to see a doctor. Go with her or have another trusted family member do it if she needs that sort of support. Thinking that there might be some brain deterioration is extremely frightening to all of us. Maybe that's not the problem, after all, but you need to find out. I've met several people who thought a parent had dementia when they were suffering from a Vitamin B deficiency. With proper supplementation the problem subsided, to everyone's great relief. The sooner everyone knows what's going on, the safer the whole family will be.

One or more family members will likely deny, to the end, that anyone in 'our family' could possibly have any form of dementia. This is an issue I'll deal with in more detail later. If denial is going to be a problem for your family, you might as well know it from the beginning.

People may survive for ten to twenty years, progressively less and less able to participate in the ordinary activities of daily living, perhaps eventually unable to communicate. By then, almost all they can do when they're awake is lie in bed and stare at the wall. No one wants to believe this might happen to them. No one wants to believe this might happen to a loved one, either. But advanced dementia looks exactly this way unless some underlying or acute condition takes the person's life before dementia progresses to that stage.

If you are planning to be directly involved, try to resolve the safety issues first. You might be surprised by how many there are. Anything from spoiled food in the refrigerator to steep slopes leading up to the house might cause trouble later.

Years ago, I had a conversation with a company that provided devices that might allow bedridden people to leave their bedrooms or their homes without standing up or even entirely sitting up. We discussed exits from a disabled elder's home and how I was worried that one specific elder might not have a safe exit in case of an emergency.

"You have no idea," the cheery person on the other end of the conversation told me, "how rarely anyone mentions this! Most older people living alone aren't safe in their own homes."

Hazards in the home come in a number of forms:

1. Environmental (the house is old and there's some toxic emission wafting through the premises)
2. Furniture, pets, area rugs, or other things in the house could present potential tripping hazards.
3. Mechanical (needed equipment—furnaces, kitchen appliances—aren't working) or there's a fault in the electrical system.
4. It isn't possible to get the place cleaned well enough, frequently enough.
5. Spoiled food remains in the refrigerator, where your loved one might eat it.

6. Medical (if no one is there to dispense medication or your loved one can't remember to take it, or perhaps accidentally overdoses).
7. Calling for help (at some point your loved one might not remember how, even if the call button is on a chain around their neck).
8. The mechanics of calling for help need to be worked out in advance of need.
9. Prior to COVID-19, many cities had vans delivering food to elders. The drivers would sit in their home and talk with them and give them company. The visit would also serve as a welfare check. There's no telling exactly when that safety check will be in full operation again. The elder care industry is still facing severe workforce shortages.[38]

Here's an unusual hazard that might affect you personally. You need to keep documentation of any help you try to provide, any lists you make, and any doctors' appointments you are responsible for making (and the results, if your loved one permits you to have them). If you don't, someone might later accuse you of neglecting your mother's needs because there's no written proof that you *did* try to help.

When You Can't Prevent Trouble

Back in the nineteenth century, the care of aging family members was purely a family matter, except for the poorest who were cared for (if at all) by the state. The way these things are handled today underscores our modern understanding that the stresses of everyday living often lead to burnout. "Caregiver burnout is a state of physical, emotional, and mental exhaustion," declares The Cleveland Clinic.[39]

Now we seem to live in a perpetual state of crisis.

If your family is contentious and you are the caregiver, you'll probably get your share of Monday morning quarterbacking. They weren't on the field, but they're eager to tell you how you should've played the game. Whether you clue the other interested parties into your plans before trouble strikes is your decision.

Some family members might come up with suggestions that might save time and improve everyone's life. And that way, they can all have input and maybe feel more included. In other families, telling relatives and friends your ideas might simply lead them to insist that you do things their way. This brings us back to the question of whether they have a 'right' to an opinion.

The federal or state government will become your employer if one of those entities gets involved. That will happen if you are receiving some government agency's help in providing care. For-profit and nonprofit agencies exist that work as 'representative payees' for Medicaid, VA, and Social Security payments. They make their living this way. The state might pay them on a per-person basis, as well. If Social Security and Medicaid payments are all the money your loved one has, they can tell the state that they can do a better, more efficient job than you are doing.

State agencies and the private ones will (and are supposed to) monitor your performance. If there are other interested parties, they will, too. Keep good records, as required by the state. And if you're required to keep others in the loop, make sure to do so.

The principals of two New Mexico commercial entities are now in prison for stealing from their wards. Together, they took a total of more than $15 million from poor people—Medicaid, Social Security, VA pensions, and the assets in handicapped trusts, as well as the money the State of New Mexico paid them for caring for these people. If your loved one has money, you can add serious greed as a motive—both on the part of would-be commercial guardians and conservators, and sometimes on the part of heirs—into the mix.

Regardless of how much you decide to collaborate with other family members, once a diagnosis of dementia or incompetence is in the 'system,' you are no longer alone in caring for your loved one. Federal guidelines (through Medicare and Medicaid) and the states (through their own programs of respite, financial compensation, training, and supervision for family caregivers) can now second-guess your formal plans to care for your loved one. They can evaluate your loved one while you are taking needed respite from your duties, or even in your home while you're doing the caregiving.

You may be required to file written statements of what you will do if emergency situations arise. The state can then evaluate your performance. Remember: once you are being paid to do a job or being given anything at all by a government or private entity, you need to expect your job performance to be judged by your benefactor.

This might even be true if your loved one has money and the court says it's fine for you to be paid privately as the caregiver. You have a contract with your loved one to provide care and are being paid out of that person's accounts. The state might designate a social worker or other person it trusts to monitor whether you're performing your job properly. Technically, you'd be working for your loved one, but that person is incapacitated and can't judge your job performance. So, an outside evaluator might be imposed on you, particularly if there are other interested parties. And here I mean other potential heirs. Even if you're the only heir, the state may still have a voice in what you do.

Another note here. Sometimes, states will accept claims in probate court against the estate of a deceased ward if the family member was caring for the assets of a person. Sometimes the figure suggested is five percent of the income, plus five percent of the expenses for the three years preceding the death of the person. An attorney can tell you whether this is true in your jurisdiction. Might a trust allow this too? You can certainly ask.

Commercial guardians are taught to keep detailed files of "just in case" procedures. They review and update these periodically. These files protect the paid caregivers in case questions are asked later. But the files only protect them if they follow their own plans. If you make such plans, it's a good idea to review them, at least annually. If your loved one's condition changes, do another review as soon as possible and document it in your own file. Document, too, that you are following doctor's orders. Again, this is a legal protection for you.

You plan in advance, for the same reason that we used to have fire drills in school. And it's the same reason the police, fire department, and military have periodic training exercises. You must know what to do 'just in case.' The time to be wondering *what do I do now?* is not when you and your loved one are in the middle of a life-or-death situation.

One of the first things living wills and 'values histories' ask is whether a person wants what's called 'full code.' That is, if they stop breathing or their heart stops, do they want medical personnel to try to start these organs working again? Sometimes, this requires using active and invasive procedures that might break bones.

If you're just the caregiver, you might realize that the house is no longer safe for your loved one to stay in and there's nothing you can do about it. The person in charge might be a commercial guardian who refuses to do the renovation work. Most states will not inspect private homes, particularly if a legal guardian is involved. Some say they will only inspect group homes—homes that care for three or more unrelated adults—but often they only regulate larger institutions.

In other words, your loved one would have to be living in a larger nursing home for them to consider inspecting the premises. One adult only child, with a mother under commercial guardianship, worried that her mother was being kept in unsafe conditions in her own home. The police and the fire department and the district attorney's office all told her, "Go to court and sue if you don't like what the legal guardian is doing!"

Then there are the other sorts of emergencies. If the ward needs oxygen and uses a concentrator, does everyone know where the backup tanks are in case the concentrator malfunctions? You should also have made plans in case the area needs to be evacuated for any reason (sewer break, gas line break, etc.). Do you have or need a back-up generator?

You might have a personal emergency yourself. Who will cover for you?

If you've been considering taking over the care of an incapacitated loved one, including a spouse (particularly if there are children or stepchildren or siblings of your loved one in the mix), now is the time to think about how their beliefs and wishes might impact you and your incapacitated loved one. Please take some time now to think about this.

Emergency medical personnel arriving at an elder's home will look for the presence of a DNR (Do Not Resuscitate) or a DNI (Do Not Intubate) order first. They will know this because it's part of their dispatch instructions. These generally say the equivalent of (and I'm giving this information in English and not EMS-speak), "emergency heart problem at this address, victim is a ninety-year-old male."

Some people might post a 'full code' order instead. But the usual fallback position has been for medical personnel to do everything possible to keep the patient alive. Sometimes, people post more than one order containing the same instructions. Perhaps they will put one in an envelope with the four-inch-high letters "DNR" or "DNI" in red on the front, one on the refrigerator in the kitchen, and another in a clear plastic sleeve of the sort you used to put photos in (back when there were physical photo albums) in the bedroom, attached to the wall directly behind and above the headboard. This is done to make sure the ambulance personnel see it.

Some guardians go to great lengths to induce a judge to order them to post a DNR order, even though this might conflict with the religious beliefs of their ward. It took years for one commercial guardian to convince the judge to 'instruct' the firm to post a DNR for a specific ward. They insisted that this had always been what that person had wanted, although her entire family only saw and heard her say repeatedly, over many years, that 'full code' was her preference.

If you are going to be the legal guardian, whether to post a DNR is one of the first things to determine. Another thing to check carefully is whether any government or private program in which you're participating requires a DNR/DNI order before they agree to provide services. (Some hospices require a DNR order on file.) And if people in your family are going to argue with you, in my opinion they might just as well do that at the beginning.

If your family tends to argue a lot, you'll need documentation that what you are saying is truly the will of your loved one and that no coercion was involved. If your family members disagree, the court is unlikely to name you as the guardian, unless you're rich or very famous and can make your competitors look bad to the judge. (Not a good strategy if you want to have an ongoing family relationship.)

Other health issues naturally arise too. Just one example: even if they take flu shots every year, some people still get the flu. Older people can dehydrate quickly. How sick does your loved one have to be, and for how long, before you'll call the ambulance?

There should be specific criteria. I once saw photocopied instructions from a doctor who made house calls to elderly homebound patients. The sheet said not to bother her unless the patient had had a fever and had been unable to eat for at least twenty-four hours. You might not like having the paramedics come, and your loved one might not like that either. However, if you don't act in a timely way with someone under your care, you risk being accused of neglect or worse.

Why might someone question you or even try to take your loved one out of your care if you make what they consider a 'wrong choice' in the care of your loved one? Hospitals and medical practitioners are taught to look for abuse by family members. If you are a family caregiver and they can interpret something you did, or avoided doing, as abuse, most likely they will.

More than twenty years ago, this scenario played out in a doctor's waiting room. A daughter was waiting for her mother to come out after her consultation with the doctor. The person sitting next to her had seen Mama go into the doctor's consulting room. Because the daughter had a darker complexion than her mother, the other woman assumed that the person one seat over was a paid caregiver like her, and not the patient's daughter. After a few moments, she decided to strike up a conversation.

"They're lucky to have us!" she started.

"Really?"

"Well, you know what they teach us. Family always gonna abuse 'em."

My experience is that this was and is the attitude all the way up the medical and psychological and legal chain of command. In my opinion, the court usually assumes that your loved ones need to be protected from you. It might take years after COVID-19, after everyone has witnessed the negative effects of isolation from friends and family, until doctors, nurses, and the legal system might admit that perhaps you play a positive role in your loved one's life, even if you don't agree with them 100 percent of the time. But then again, maybe some of these folks never will.

Think back to the fact that the state and the federal government have essentially become your employers if you are receiving some government agency's help in providing care. Remember, too, that commercial agencies might choose to tell the state that they can do a better job. My guess is that the state will listen to them because they are experts in the field, but you are only a family member.

Always remind yourself that these state agencies and the private ones to which they habitually refer cases are watching your performance. Just to repeat this important information: if there are other interested parties, they will be, too.

States might be monitoring contracts incapacitated elders might make with family caregivers. Check on the current requirements in your state before agreeing to do this work. This is not high-paying employment. You will not be paid more than the going rate in your area for the services you provide. Even if your loved one is paying you 'privately' to do the work, the state might decide to send someone to check on your performance. This becomes more likely when more money, entitlement money, and other potential heirs are involved.

The situation in which one sibling becomes the caregiver and the rest of the grown children have no part in their parent's day-to-day life is likely to activate any long-dormant intra-family rivalries, so beware. If there is any or dissension, the state is likely to swoop in and declare that someone of their choosing can do a better job. They believe your loved one needs a calm environment.

Now, we've reviewed what sorts of emergency plans you need, and how to make them. The next thing you need to consider is whether there are people on whom you can rely.

Relying on Others

The states are showing an increasing tendency to take over incapacitated people in ways that remind me of an episode called "The Changeling" from the 1967 season of *Star Trek*. Something has gone terribly wrong with a powerful space probe. Its programming has been corrupted. Instead of examining and analyzing soil samples, it has come to believe that its mission is to destroy all life forms that are not perfect.

This new, defective programming makes the device highly dangerous as it travels the universe, turning its death rays on seemingly all life forms in its path (because all of them have some flaw or another). Future potential victims are saved when Mr. Spock and Captain Kirk find a way to convince the probe that it is flawed itself, at which point it self-destructs.

If your family life doesn't conform to some expert's idea of perfection—and perfection appears to mean that no one ever disagrees with anyone else—then they are going to prevent you from having any interaction or control unless what you do is perfect according to their standards. They might not realize that when one family member suffers from dementia, or is otherwise incapacitated, the others who don't are likely to disagree, at least sometimes. If they always agreed with the thinking of a demented person, they'd have to be demented, also.

This sort of illogical demand has led commercial guardians to allow family members to discuss only carefully selected topics with their loved one, provided they're allowed to visit at all. (Granted, certain topics and certain sorts of questions might upset or confuse a person with dementia. That's not what I'm talking about.)

In an excess of zeal, some guardians dictate that their ward never be upset, even at funerals. Don't laugh! One guardian told her ward's daughter that her mother could attend her son-in-law's funeral, "but only if she doesn't get upset."

If guardianship hearings continue to be conducted in secret, and if the courts continue to insist that families whose members aren't always in perfect harmony shouldn't be allowed to care for their elders, the frequency with which judges will give family members with dementia into the control of commercial guardians will only increase. My friends who have had a divorce involving child custody in their background often report similar unrealistic requirements.

Periodically, reports of commercial guardians abusing their wards surface. They lead to bad publicity for that industry. Sometimes, the miscreants are sentenced to jail. All agencies involved in the care of people who have been separated from their families seem to be rocked by periodic scandals.

In April 2023, the State of New Mexico agreed to bring in an outside evaluator to monitor the treatment of developmentally disabled adults and children under the state's care. Why? An adult developmentally disabled woman had died in the care of a corporation, under circumstances the New Mexico Attorney General described as "torture."[40] The outside investigators uncovered many more suspected cases.

Several times since 1986, Congress has held hearings because so many reports of abuse in the guardianship process were published during a relatively short period. What was the outcome each time? Well, considering that Congress has been accepting the commercial guardianship industry's statistics, it's hardly surprising that these hearings have led to ever-stricter requirements for family guardians, but at a state rather than a federal level. Because, ultimately, the states have the power to regulate this industry.

Here's one example: On January 15, 2021, the New Mexico Supreme Court announced that, as of February 1, all people who wanted to serve as guardians or conservators would be required to watch a series of videos detailing their duties and responsibilities under the law. What did this do? Well, for one thing, currently certified commercial guardians wouldn't need to watch those videos again because they would have already passed an examination on the material contained in them. To this, the Supreme Court added another requirement that all prospective guardians or conservators file a sworn statement five days prior to any competency hearing in which they attest to having already viewed all the relevant videos.

In most cases, this seems reasonable. However, sometimes an 'emergency guardianship' is needed. A person is unconscious, in the hospital, and someone must be found to make immediate decisions. As of July 2021, the videos were still not on the court's website. They were hidden away with other videos on other topics somewhere in YouTubeville. In an emergency situation, a family whose members had not already seen the videos would not have time to file anything "five days in advance of the hearing."

Either the judge must grant an extension to the family member or a commercial entity must take over, because that unconscious person needs immediate help. Someone must make decisions, sign documents, etc. Who will serve as guardian during that period? Almost certainly a commercial guardian. Who will test family members to see that they know the material? Most likely, the courts, advised by commercial guardians, will eventually devise some sort of exam. If they fail, it's reasonable to assume that the loved one will continue under the supervision of a commercial entity.

If they do pass the exam and take over the right to care for their loved one, who will supervise them? Why, the same commercial guardians and other professionals in related industries, of course! The guardians and their expensive attorneys and lobbyists are well organized, and they all have at their disposal the money they earned from caring for earlier wards or from representing the guardians in legal combat.

The families of wards have no such powerful national organization. A few groups are now trying to help family members, but these are generally small and specialized in their approaches to the problem. The Life Legal Defense Foundation, for instance, only represents families disputing those who want to withhold food and drink or life-saving care from their loved ones.[41]

To be fair, sometimes, a family guardian does something wrong, too, but usually only to one person at a time. A family guardian with one ward can't harm people on a grand scale, and certainly not on the same scale as a commercial guardian, who might abuse 200 human beings at a time. Some commercial guardianship firms handle more than that number of wards annually.

What a family guardian can do 'wrong' ranges from forgetting to file the required reports to moving. Moving a ward to the next county, or even the home down the street, requires prior approval from the court. If you move the ward without telling the court and getting a judge to sign off on the change, you might well lose the right to remain your loved one's guardian. If your loved one is living in a facility and you want to move her to another facility, again you might need court approval first.

The more educational requirements and regulations the jurisdiction where your loved one lives has governing a family member who becomes the guardian, the more carefully you must observe the details. Document major medical events as well as income and expenses. Commercial guardians track visitors and any number of other things, including the contents of meals and how much water a specific ward drinks in a day. Be sure to find out, in advance, exactly what your loved one's jurisdiction requires.

How would you know, in advance, that a course at a senior center on solving family conflicts is being offered by a commercial guardian whose firm might be using that class to prospect for new clients? Unless you do very careful research, you wouldn't. And if your state keeps those court dockets secret, you'll have a very hard time finding this information. More than a couple of people have confided in just such an instructor with a conflict of interest. It's relatively easy for someone with a psychology background to increase strife instead of defusing it, and then to swoop in as the pretend protector of the elder in this situation.

Any professional whose income stream might be increased by having more control over your loved one might have ulterior motives. But then, again, people also might, perfectly innocently, become worried and report that a person might need a welfare check or might be having trouble in some area of life, even if they don't stand to benefit financially in any way. A person's good intentions can't guarantee a good outcome from either your point of view or your loved one's.

Some years ago, a friend of mine put two of her relatives with dementia into a small nursing home. She had been caring for them in her own home. She wanted to prevent someone from the respite care agency she knew she'd have to hire, if they remained at home with her, from reporting their whereabouts to the commercial guardian of another relative of hers. Because she didn't live in a large city, she was afraid that any paid service coming to her home might act similarly.

Why did she do this? She knew that she couldn't work 24/7 and was sure that someday a commercial service would be able to find something they imagined she was doing wrong and take her relatives away. Putting them in a home in advance was the only way she could think of to ensure her ability to visit them whenever possible.

Given that this sort of 'spiriting away' of a relative by a commercial guardian had already happened in her family, I couldn't really say that her anxiety was excessive. As it turned out, the nursing home administrator agreed to keep her relatives' presence at the home a secret. She refrained from posting their names on the door to their room, and they spent the rest of their lives in peace. My friend managed the whole situation with her powers of attorney, executed when those two relatives were fully competent. She also did not have any relatives willing to go to court to challenge her.

I've met a few official 'family guardians.' One man, acting as a family caregiver for his mother who had dementia, looked perpetually anxious. We started discussing what he'd learned in his adult caregiving class offered by a local nonprofit specializing in dementia issues. "You aren't allowed to argue with 'em," he volunteered. "It's the biggest thing. They can do and say anything, and you always have to say, 'Yes!'"

Anyone can imagine situations—including crossing a street against the light—when allowing patients to do what they want might kill them.

Some family members may cause seemingly insoluble problems because of actions they take in what they believe is their own self-interest. One of them consults an attorney or social worker about any problems in the family relationship. If those professionals aren't scrupulously honest, they may promise the family troublemaker that she'll become the guardian if she'll (usually it's a 'she') only sue for guardianship. Her parent has dementia, or is otherwise incapacitated, and others in the situation might have some old rivalry or jealousy issues with her.

An attorney or other trusted professional might already know about family strife. A tipoff is that certain close relatives might not appear in a person's will or trust, or they might be specifically disinherited, suggesting already existing estrangement between them. Or they are not named as powers of attorney (POAs) in any of the potential ward's legal papers.

What happens when this matter comes before a judge? "There's dissension in this family," one of the court-appointed experts reports. "I worry that, if one of these people becomes guardian, she'll bar the others from visiting."

Regardless of what that expert might have promised (verbally, but generally not in writing) to the person brought in to create that conflict, standard court practice for decades has been to place the ward in a situation where that person is 'insulated' against any possible upset.

"This person is fragile and needs protection from the internal family conflict," the judge then declares. "Normally, the daughter would become the guardian, but in this case, I rule that this is not in the best interests of the ward."

Regardless of any oral promises an expert might have made before the hearing, the parent generally goes into the hands of a commercial guardian, never to emerge during this lifetime. I've seen this sort of action drive what appears to be the final spike into the heart of that family as a unit. Even for some of those families, there might be a later remedy. I'll go further into that in Chapter VII.

An alternate scenario is for a concerned family member who genuinely wants to protect an endangered elder to start guardianship proceedings. Any actor in the scenario who has questionable motives and some appearance of power in the court process may then manipulate one or more other interested persons. Either they are promised more power over the situation, or possibly a large inheritance as the prize, if they simply try to destroy the credibility of the first person. Perhaps the expert can reignite an old rivalry or resentment. Hired caregivers are not exempt from taking sides in these conflicts and can further complicate the situation.

The third frequent variation on this theme is for the court experts to find two family members (or other interested parties in the matter) who have never gotten along well and have the judge agree to appoint them joint guardians for a probationary period. They will find out where dissention exists through interviews that are required by the court during the guardianship creation process.

Any requirements placed on the newly-appointed people will equal or exceed those that would normally be imposed on a commercial guardian acting within a large guardianship firm. This means a lot of convoluted record-keeping and all sorts of long-in-advance activity planning that family members don't normally do. Never having resolved their own former tensions, the two guardians' joint efforts fail, ending with a, "See, I told you family members can't do this job!" attitude reinforced on the part of both the judge and the experts.

If you know enough about the social relationships of the experts involved, that might help too. In one case I analyzed, a major guardianship attorney was the domestic partner of someone working for an important guardianship firm. In that case, it probably wouldn't have been a good idea to go to the attorney to complain about that guardianship firm. You might have more trouble identifying this sort of relationship in a large city, but it might save you an incredible amount of grief if you can manage to do it.

Conclusion

We've just discussed why a family relationship does not necessarily confer any special legal powers or decision-making capabilities on the members, as well as how and why state agencies feel they have a right to tell family members what to do, and how documents intended to make clear a ward's wishes may be either falsified or misconstrued. Being a caregiver is very different from having a court-granted capacity to make decisions. In the next chapter, we'll concentrate on various issues relating to finances.

TAKEAWAYS

1. There's a major difference between being a guardian and being a caregiver.
2. Be sure you know when, where, and under what circumstances a 'values document' was created.
3. If you plan to become a caregiver, check into the state requirements to protect both yourself and your loved one.
4. Realize that accepting money from the state or from another organization might entitle them to monitor your performance in various ways.

CHAPTER V
What Does It Cost?
The Money and Who Takes It

Have you wondered why—in addition to the explanations I've already given you—people so often end up broke during retirement? You'll finish Chapter V understanding why that's so common. And also what some of the negative results of relying on agents and powers of attorney might be.

Baby Boomers started reaching age sixty-five in 2009, a year after the federal government raised the age for receiving full Social Security benefits to sixty-six.

The last of the Baby Boomers will reach sixty-five in 2031, but by then the 'retirement age' will be sixty-seven. As Baby Boomers pass on, if there are any remaining assets, their money and possessions then go either to the people named in their wills or as beneficiaries of their trusts, or to people named in state law (if they die without a will). If there's enough money, the federal and/or state government will step in, demanding the payment of taxes. The definition of a taxable estate varies over time.

Many of those assets might already, as many people suspect, often go to others of the legal system's choosing before that person dies. Will there be anything left for those for whom the person who wrote those wills and set up those trusts intended to provide? For people with no possessions, the state will still pay for the wind-up of their 'estates' and for their burial or cremation, so someone will still get paid.

Here's an example: About that New Jersey ward I mentioned earlier, the one who died in 2020 and had no money, the State of New Jersey had paid for the ward's final arrangements without consulting his family. The state had also paid the state-appointed guardian to make these arrangements before anyone even contacted his adult children. Did New Jersey do what the ward wanted? Who knows?

After you finish this chapter, you'll know where the money is going. Then, you'll be able to assess whether there's anyone you can trust. You'll have a basis to judge to what extent the law might (or might not) be able to help you, and to figure out whether you might be able to salvage any of the items from your past that you value.

Money (or the Lack of It) and the Elder Care System

Many members of the middle class are being squeezed dry in the process of this wealth transfer. In my opinion, a great number of those with assets of $1-4 million will be, too. The poor will suffer in a slightly different way, because their caregivers are appointed and usually paid by the state, but they are equally powerless unless they know what's happening.

Anyone who's ever been involved in the elder care system can readily confirm that money seems to evaporate like a shallow pool of water in the desert sun. Some of the demographic reasons are built into the system. There are simply fewer children in the United States than there used to be. The Baby Boomers had fewer children than the Great Generation (their parent's generation).

Children in traditional societies were expected to share the responsibility of caring for their elders. Extended families often lived in the same town or a neighboring town. They might even have lived together in the same home. A nuclear family might have included six people—two parents and four children. Sometimes one of the children stayed home and dedicated a lifetime to caring for aging parents.

We don't live in a traditional society anymore, so that rarely happens today. Our problems are rapidly worsening as we become a nation where fewer children and close relatives live near the elder and increasing numbers of self-described or court-appointed 'experts' emerge, compounded by more and more people in need of caregiving. Our society is aging.

Someone in your life might need help, either now or in the future. I'll talk about what choices you and your loved ones do have. Maybe there's a way to protect them and, with some attention and effort, you and your other loved ones, as well.

What's a Nest Egg? How Far Does It Go?

The nineteenth-century American philosopher and author Ralph Waldo Emerson is credited with being the first person to say "health is wealth." It's also true that if you lose your health, you are most likely to lose your wealth, as well. Unfortunately, most people discover, too late, that ignorance is not bliss. In fact, quite the opposite.

As people age, they tend to use more of their money for medical services. Estimates of how much a retired couple will spend for *normal* healthcare, beyond what Medicare pays, range from CNBC's $390,000 to *US News and World Report's* October 2020 statement that the average is $285,000. By 2023, the website The Annuity Expert estimated the cost had risen to $295,000 *per person.*[42]

These figures are for otherwise healthy people, and do not include any of the expenses of staying in an extended-care setting, like assisted living. So, a couple retiring now with a nest egg of $300,000 in cash can expect to spend almost all of it (if not even more than their total savings) on routine medical care, providing inflation doesn't exhaust it sooner. Then, too, some people need more medical care than others.

Medicare kicks in at about age sixty-five, but according to the Bureau of the Census, about 15 percent of people aged sixty-five to sixty-nine are in debt because of their medical bills. This percentage falls to about 10 percent between ages seventy to seventy-four, and after that, levels off at about 8 percent.[43]

It's unclear whether the census people consider home health aides to be part of a senior's 'medical expenses.' Medicare doesn't pay for them at all. If the government included the percentages of seniors owing money because of this specific expense, they might be reporting a far higher percentage of seniors in debt over medical issues than their statistics now show.

Those who require someone else to make all major decisions for them must have not only medical care, but also some sort of companion with them 24/7. Failing that, they need to live in a facility that has such caregivers on staff, which greatly increases their expenses.

Back in 2006, it cost $100,000 to keep one man in an Albuquerque nursing home for about eighteen months before he was able to return home on hospice care (and with one private-duty attendant). By 2020, one inflation calculation website estimated that this $100,000 would have increased to over $129,000. By 2023, the true amount should have been between $144,704 (according to Smart Asset) and $153,598.85 (according to the Minneapolis Federal Reserve). They both claim to be using the same method of calculation, so what accounts for the almost $9,000 difference?

So, beware of the convenience of using these sites to project. If your budget is tight, that difference might be enough to destroy even the best-laid plans.

Home care is even more expensive. After the man I just mentioned returned home to hospice in 2007, the cost rose to $11,000 for one month of having a single aide with him 24/7. So, in 2024, that would have cost just over $16,634. Every month. That's $199,608 in a year. A practical nurse came once or twice a week as part of hospice. Her services were free. The cost of the aides didn't include food or laundry or the expenses of running the house, either. Caregiving expenses vary with the services needed and the area of the country.[44]

Long-term care insurance will help a lot, at least for a while. This man didn't have it, nor did the woman I mentioned earlier who had more than one aide per shift. Many younger people now find they are rejected by long-term care insurers if they have a pre-existing condition.

Using Genworth as an example, their annual premiums formerly cost about $9,000. That had been true for years, but in May 2023, all their long-term care policyholders got an unwelcome surprise.

The company had discovered that too many people were living "too long" (from the insurer's point of view) while collecting payouts on their policies. This situation was causing the company to lose money. If it continued, they would have to discontinue the program. They offered their clients these options:

1. Pay the premium when the next bill arrives (with a 2024 premium of $11,267.20). This option would include unlimited lifetime benefits but offer no cap on premium increases.
2. Two alternative options within this second category kept a stable premium but cut benefits to a lifetime limit of just over $433,000, with limited inflation protection (for a 2024 annual premium of $4,791.78).
3. Two greatly reduced coverage options in this category allowed additional further reviews of both coverage and costs, with annual premiums running between just over

$6,000 and a maximum of just over $8,600 per year. (Each year, you would be faced with complex decisions.)

Now, let's go back to the couple retiring with a $300,000 nest egg. In about two years, long-term care expenses alone would exhaust all the remaining cash for a person without that insurance. If one couple member had the $433,000 policy coverage, another few years of home care would likely entirely exhaust both that benefit and the remaining cash. And remember: the insurance company may place restrictions on who provides the care. Must the caregivers be licensed? Certified? It's their call. The more qualifications, the greater the per-hour rate and the faster your payout cap will be reached.

Basic Medicare doesn't cover dental care at all. To get that service, you'd need to buy a separate dental policy or pay your bills with your nest egg.

Does Your Loved One Have Money Issues?

Many members of the Greatest Generation and the Baby Boom Generation started their own businesses. Often, their families saw this family-owned business as being both their livelihood and their inheritance. But once the founder begins to fail, often the business does, too. If the founder owns 51 percent of the business and a guardian is appointed, the guardian will now be making business decisions. Will a person's court-appointed commercial guardian be an expert in that business? Probably not.

And here's another sort of cautionary tale. One man whose business activities I followed had built a good-sized business from scratch. It grew to the point where he announced, during the 1960s, that it was worth about $70 million. That would equal just under $633 million today. He decided to sell out and enjoy retirement—with the understanding that Henry, his longtime second-in-command, would pay the acquisition fee over time out of the income from that business.

The problem was that Henry was used to taking orders, not giving them. Revenue fell steeply, cutting into the former owner's retirement income. Within two years, he had taken the business over again and was still running it in 1987. He ran it up until the day he died. Had he developed dementia, he wouldn't have been able to do that, and the business likely would have failed. Despite his millions, this man never got to enjoy retirement.

As for family businesses, in general, selling them rarely brings in the money people expect, providing they can be sold at all. The more closely the founder is identified with the business, the harder it is to sell or to keep it running. According to Worldwide Business Brokers, only 20 percent of businesses with assets of $1 million or less can be sold, and only 30 percent of those with assets between $1 million and $100 million are ultimately salable.[45]

When family members watch a court-appointed guardian selling the ward's assets for pennies on the dollar, sometimes they're furious, thinking the guardian is trying to pauperize the family. Perhaps that's true sometimes, but this also might happen because when there's a distress sale to raise assets to care for the ward, everything must be sold at a discount.

Does your loved one seem to have money issues now? If bills suddenly go unpaid, there might be many reasons, ranging from insufficient income after retirement to cover amounts easily paid before, to memory problems (forgetting to pay the bills), to someone you may never have met siphoning money out of a person's accounts.

Many families never discuss finances. Or, members of the family don't seem to trust other members enough to confide financial information. Someone must start the discussion as soon as possible, but perhaps when the family is sitting around a festive dinner table, it might not be the optimal time to do this. Meeting family members online might allow everyone to have the comfort of familiar surroundings when discussing this topic.

Was your loved one always gullible? People easily taken in by others earlier in life are likely to be at even greater risk as they age, particularly if they have become isolated and crave company. Social groups and churches abound with people wanting to fleece elders by befriending them, gaining their trust, then taking their assets. We even have names for this: elder fraud and affinity fraud. Some family members are equally capable of this unsavory activity.

Political parties are also culpable. "Hundreds of elderly political donors, some of them with dementia, have fallen victim to Republican and Democratic political campaigns and groups," declared CNN toward the end of the Presidential Campaign season in 2024.[46]

My apologies for mentioning this, but even houses of worship sometimes look as if they may be guilty of affinity fraud. I've heard of one that routinely recommended only a single trust attorney. It turned out that he was also an elder of the large congregation. Congregants who elected not to use his services found themselves criticized or ostracized.

It can get even worse. An elderly couple related to a friend of mine attended a 'legacy planning seminar' years ago. (For convenience, I'll call the husband "Bill.") The home office of their sect was urging members to create charitable trusts, using the church's legal division as their trustee. The trusts would pay out income to the named beneficiaries for their lifetime. After they passed away, what remained would go as a gift to the church. Attorneys hired by the church stood in the back of the room, papers and notaries at the ready. It was, the organizers told attendees, "the best, most devout use of your money."

Bill had already retired from a top corporate position. Estimates of his net worth ranged from $20 million to $100 million. All the attendees were watching Bill, expecting him to sign. Pressure? You bet!

After the couple left the meeting, the husband started having second thoughts. The church hadn't given him copies of any of the documents he'd executed that day. Bill wasn't an attorney and had barely had a chance to skim over the papers before he signed them. He called the home office, requesting that they send him copies.

The church continued to delay sending him these papers despite repeated requests, so Bill hired an independent attorney. The new attorney then requested, from the home church's legal department, copies of every document his new client had signed for the church.

Instead of sending the documents, the church did something entirely different: it argued that the trusts Bill had created must stand because they believed Bill must have become mentally incompetent during the few intervening months, in fact so mentally incapacitated that he now needed a guardian.

From the church's point of view, Bill had originally made the most prudent decision possible. He'd picked the church as trustee. If he had any later misgivings, they reasoned, it must be due to this new mental defect they now claimed that Bill had developed, or to some other person's undue influence.

The church already had total control of all Bill's assets; a judge allowed them to administer the trusts until after Bill's wife died, at which time, all remaining assets became the property of that religious institution. The same judge also gave Bill himself into the control of a commercial guardianship firm. After that, no family member had any power to influence events, not even Bill's wife.

This attitude isn't limited to churches. I've even seen other nonprofits try to demand an amount of money named in a will from the executor, ignoring the inconvenient fact that the person who wrote the will had died without assets sufficient to pay that bequest.

Retired elders who always managed their own finances well earlier in life now have the knowledge and time to play with their money. The question is: do they want to? Are they still actively working with their own finances? Have they, perhaps, passed on that work to someone else? Who now has the power to control their finances?

If possible, meet that person. You'll need your loved one's permission to do this; ethical money managers and investment advisors won't want to see you about an elder's account unless you have power of attorney or are designated in their paperwork as a person entitled to such information. Often, they require the first meeting to include the owner of the account.

Your loved one might be far more of a risk-taker or far more risk-averse than you. If their attitude has changed radically recently, and they can't articulate why (and neither can their financial adviser), you might have reason to be concerned. I'll be saying more about that possibility later in this chapter.

Taxes might be an issue also. Money withdrawn from retirement accounts might be entirely taxable. Do you think taxes went up or down since your loved one deposited the money there? Shortly before COVID-19 struck, a few financial planners had begun to admit, in public, that the 4 percent withdrawals they had been telling people to remove from their retirement accounts annually to live on were leading half of these retirees to run out of money during their lifetime.[47] Financial planners have been recommending this '4 percent-per-year withdrawal plan' for more than thirty years.

Here's another problem most people don't expect: Baby Boomers were taught to try to buy homes. For some reason, they were also fed the line that their home should be their most expensive possession, the grandest they could possibly find and get a loan to buy. If the mortgage is paid off, it ties up all that value in one asset. But, if it's not paid off, a lot of money goes to the bank or the mortgage company monthly. And this investment provides absolutely no income.

Mortgaging a house might create a stack of cash. However, if there's a mortgage, then there's also a large debt to pay off. That only works in your favor if you can make more money yourself than you're paying monthly on the mortgage. Most people were taught that real estate can only appreciate in value. However, as we know from the real estate crisis of 2007-08, a home may also lose value.

Homes come with built-in expenses—real estate taxes, insurance, and upkeep. There's a very good chance that the real estate tax will have at least doubled if a couple has lived in the same place for many years. Here's an example: in Bernalillo County, New Mexico, real estate taxes rise about 3 percent annually. So, let's say someone moved into a home there in 1997. Those taxes would have more than doubled by 2021. Many of today's elders moved into their current homes in the 1980s and 90s.

Just to be clear, this is a logarithmic increase. If the tax was $10,000 in 1997, it would be $10,030 (3 percent higher) in 1998. Then, the next increase would be $10,300.90, (3 percent more than was paid in 1998). And so on through the years.

The Tax Foundation has an illuminating handout showing that real estate taxes didn't rise as much in some places as in others during that period. The average tax increase was 4 percent per year during 2007-09.[48] Given recent economic developments, many counties, states, and cities need even more money than before COVID-19. Where will that come from? Most likely from a further increase in property (and other) tax rates.

Any other loans (including credit card bills and car payments) factor into this calculation, too. So many people are buying on credit things they can't afford to purchase for cash. And they are doing so at enormous interest rates. According to Debt.org, someone with a credit score between 670 and 739 will likely pay, as of 2024, an interest rate in the 20-22 percent range.[49]

That's for someone with a little better-than-average credit. So, let's say a couple has $30,000 in debt at 20 percent interest. If they pay back $1,000/month, it will take them forty-two months to pay back everything they owe. And they'll also end up paying an additional $11,935 in interest.[50] (A few short years ago, the interest payment would have been about $7,600.) Meanwhile, they'll also have to live, which means buying food and clothing while they're paying off the existing debt. Will they buy those other things on credit, too?

Years ago, the State of New York required an incapacitated elder's court-appointed guardian to take, in annual payment, a certain percentage of the ward's income and expenses. The more money flowing into and out of the ward's accounts, the larger the guardian's annual fee. Other states have other arrangements.

If a private aide costs $19.95/hour in your locality, and your loved one needs this sort of care 24/7, that's $478.80/day. You are looking at $175,000/year. But wait! You often must pay workers double-time on holidays. How many holidays does your loved one's home care service recognize? If you're paying someone privately, will that person be classified by the IRS as an employee? More on the ramifications of that later.

Social Security payments, rather than continuing to rise with inflation, will likely be cut by 25 percent before 2031. Since 2022, the cost of living (COLA) increases have declined steeply. Elders with nest eggs and taxable income might lose more, based precisely on the fact that they have nest eggs and taxable income. Those with family members who have been receiving Social Security Disability benefits are likely to see payments shrink even before 2031.

Now, about 25 percent of that Social Security pension goes to pay for Medicare insurance. That's off the top before the retirees even see that money.

COVID-19 made things worse. What working people were paying in to Social Security was already less than the amount the government paid out. But the people who are continuing to pay in are still not contributing as much as Social Security pays out.

Some states charge tax on Social Security payments, as well.

In January 2020, Congress passed the Secure Act. What it "secured" was the government's right to tax all the assets contained in inherited IRAs and 401ks, and so-called IRA trusts, within ten years of the demise of the original owner. This makes bequeathing an IRA to a non-spouse or someone who is not chronically ill (these folks are exempt from that ten-year liquidation requirement) far less attractive as a tax-planning strategy. If your loved one tells you that you will inherit an IRA or other retirement account, you might want to ask some questions. This gift might increase your own tax burden considerably.

Despite repeated attempts, Congress has not yet deleted from the tax statute the so-called 'step-up' provisions that don't require heirs to pay taxes on the full increase in value of assets since their loved one bought them. But legislators repeatedly introduce these provisions. If they eventually pass, estates and heirs will owe far more in taxes than they do now, meaning that heirs will inherit far less than their loved one intended.

Although some people believe that Medicare pays for home care aides, it doesn't. I can't emphasize this enough. If your loved one won't be safe without a home health aide over a long period of time, and there's no long-term care policy (or its benefits are exhausted), the payment will have to come from the patient or the patient's family. At more than $14,880 per thirty-one-day month in Albuquerque, and a 'low rate' of about $16,000/month in New York City—to mention only two examples—money disappears rapidly. Might this expense change your goal of where a loved one should live? Remember that the home health aide is only one of the expenses.

Let's look at someone who lived for nine years after her 2003 dementia diagnosis. It never cost her less than $90,000 (including benefits, in 2003) annually for a full-time home health care worker, and in many years, more for some of the companies. For this one ward, the total expenses, as reported to the court, far surpassed $4.5 million over that same nine years.

According to the conservative numbers offered by Bureau of Labor Statistics's CPI Inflation Calculator, by July 2024, with that $90,000, adjusted for inflation, the annual expenses for health aides alone would have ballooned to more than $153,000.[51]

Some long-term care insurance policies have a cap of a million dollars. For many, as you've already seen, it's less. They might require you to pay a third of the total amount upfront. (How many people can tie up that much cash in this way over a period of years?) You've already seen what happens to long-term care premiums when people start living longer. If you ultimately need more money, perhaps for medical bills or living expenses, you'll have to get it somewhere else.

Long-term care policy providers have, as I said before, been losing money. Some have sold their long-term care insurance policy operations to other firms. A lot of those original insurance companies have well-known names. However, ultimately the person who pays the premiums has no control over who owns the policy. The company paying out on your claim might not be the same one you signed up with years earlier. And the terms of that policy might have changed substantially.

What you've just read is a bare-bones introduction to these issues.[52]

Conclusion

So, to sum up, you need to be aware of all the payments—health, living, insurance, and so on—that your loved ones might still need to make. Whenever someone tells you, "I'm all set for retirement. I've made careful plans, and I've put you in my will for $100,000," you can either try to protect their pride and say nothing, or you can tell them what I've just told you. In any case, don't count on that inheritance.

Any plans you make are a best guess scenario. So are the simulations created by an investment advisor. The scenarios they show you are simply scripts. Like a play script, they show a plot that's plausible, all other things being equal. But sometimes they're not. The next chapter talks about how people try to hang onto possessions and, if they do, what results they might expect.

TAKEAWAYS

1. What might seem like a lot of money might not be once you start figuring out the expenses.
2. Health care alone might cost more than most people have saved as their nest egg.
3. Long-term insurance might no longer be the answer, since it has become increasingly hard to get.
4. If you know the real money situation with your elders, they and you will be able to plan far better.

CHAPTER VI

Alternatives and Passing on Possessions

In this chapter, we'll explore various ways people attempt to control what happens after they die. There are many members of large and thriving professions, including financial planners, accountants, estate planners, and attorneys who try to help their clients create iron-clad wills, trusts, and other legal and financial plans that will shield their assets and protect their loved ones. They are often successful, but sometimes, for various reasons, things just don't work out as planned.

You saw this in Chapter I, when a loving patriarch's trust plan backfired, leaving his eldest son homeless and out of a job. All through *They're Coming for Your Elders and Your Inheritance*, people lost out, often after they thought they'd done everything right. Looking back on their plight, many battles could have been avoided with early and ongoing communication, a problem which we'll deal with in later chapters. But this chapter discusses what an elder might like to pass on, and how that might most efficiently be accomplished.

What Recourse Do You Have?

One New York attorney told me, "An oral contract is only as good as the paper it's written on." Another of his favorite sayings was, "You show me a contract and I'll show you how to break it."

If you've known a person for fifty years and never could trust that individual before, the chances are that you can't trust that person now.

For the most part, registered investment advisors and brokers aren't allowed to take powers of attorney over the accounts they manage. However, many of them manage investment accounts and take a percentage of the total value of the account as an annual fee. If they hold the account for thirty years, at a 2 percent fee per year, the fees alone will amount to 60 percent of the initial principal—more if the value of that account increases.

Another option is for them to act like real estate agents and take a percentage or a specific amount per share of stock you buy or sell. Some people don't like this alternative, believing that it gives them an incentive to convince you to trade more to generate extra commissions for them. Many might also be licensed to sell insurance products to supplement their income.

As I mentioned earlier, the creator of the "4 percent rule" now says the 4 percent he mentioned was the *maximum* amount to withdraw annually, and not the *optimum* amount. I'm truly sorry for all the retirees who were instructed to withdraw that 4 percent for the past twenty-five years. They followed instructions and now have no more cash in that account. No one is going to apologize for the 'error,' and no one is going to refund them that money, either.

It's far safer if someone you know you can trust is near the person who can't manage finances alone but is living 'independently.' I don't mean living with them, which might lead to charges that they are exercising undue influence. Instead, I mean seeing them frequently. As frequently as they need to be seen. Or this job might be shared among several trustworthy people. Those who can't manage their finances should not have financial information lying around the house where casual visitors might find it.

Even seemingly simple actions become far more complex (and more expensive) if an elder can't walk easily. Here's an example: people who can't walk might need ramps so they can go outside safely in a wheelchair. I'm familiar with a case, dating from the early years of this century, where no ramp was installed.

In the absence of a $200 ramp, simply going out to lunch or to a doctor's appointment required a special car service with an attendant willing to pick the elder up physically and carry both her and her wheelchair out of the house and back. Paid aides insisted that they could wheel her down a ramp, but that picking up either the client or her wheelchair, with her in it, was not part of their job description.

Each formerly simple excursion cost the elder $300. Free transportation services provided by the county required considerable advance notice, which it wasn't always possible to give. The patient was capable of transferring to a car herself with the help of her aide, so she didn't really need a handicapped van. However, in her city, that was the only service willing to carry people out of their homes.

Medicare didn't pay for those expenses. Inflation increased from $300 in 2006 to at least $466.59 in 2024.

This is one way money flies out the door.[53]

It's so easy to confuse or misinform those who are far away! People might tell you only what they think you want to hear. Your loved one needs boots on the ground.

"A body of men holding themselves accountable to nobody ought not to be trusted by anybody," Thomas Paine, one of our Founding Fathers, said.

He had intended this declaration to apply to an unelected government. Our elders under guardianship are considered wards of that secretive state. Given the string of abuses of the elderly by commercial guardians that the media has exposed since 1986, this warning seems to apply equally well to commercial guardians and conservators as well as to treatment guardians, representative payees, and trustees of people who are not mentally competent to handle their affairs.

Sometimes it's hard for a member of the general public to trust people who habitually work in adult guardianship. Their attitudes and expectations appear to come from the legal profession or from social work. Even if an action conforms to the standards or ideals of those fields, frequently it's not the way the real world has ever worked. For example, expecting family members in a crisis situation never to disagree with each other, or always to remain calm.

Judges seem to want what's called a 'stipulated agreement,' which means that everyone agrees on what to do before a case ever comes to court for a hearing. Then, the judge simply signs an 'order' that just makes it official.

This frees the judge from ever really having to judge anything, but often it also means that someone might have been pressured into making an agreement that is one-sided and favorable to the party with the highest-priced or most powerful attorneys. "Clients come and go, but colleagues are forever," I once saw a former judge write in an email to an attorney who was then being pressured to go along to get along.

You've probably heard some form of this advice already: court is a very expensive recourse to be avoided, if possible. Money disappears fast, any legal resolution seems to take forever, and the process is emotionally draining. I recently saw one state's Supreme Court congratulate itself for resolving its cases in just under two years. However, they never mentioned that all those cases had generally dragged on in district court, and then during appeals to lower courts, for years before that. If each stage took two years, we'd be talking about a six-year process, not a two-year process.

Someone reliable must have control over the assets. Friends of mine who'd seen attorneys appointed as guardians or trustees quickly realized that even if an attorney is reading the mail to his ward, he might still be charging the same hourly rate (perhaps $250 or more) as he would if he were arguing a case in court. Although this isn't supposed to be ethical, I've heard of it happening multiple times.

In ethical legal billing, the idea is to separate functions so that the client is not billed above the 'pay grade' of the expertise necessary to do the work. It would help if state laws and rules reflected this ethical situation.[54]

Judges may appoint others to investigate or even to make decisions for them without the need (from their point of view) for a court hearing. Although the state pays the judge, the ward always pays these other people who might be called 'guardians ad litem' or 'special masters,' or perhaps something else, depending on their degree of authority and the state where the events are taking place. Hearings have transcripts where people must go 'on the record,' and sometimes even testify under oath. A decision made by a special master is generally arrived at without a hearing. This means there's no reliable paper trail. A guardian ad litem or a special master will be on the record when submitting reports to a judge.

My book *Protecting Mama* explains in detail how many functionaries were appointed by the court and paid, using my mother's funds, during—and even after—my mother's guardianship. The more of them are involved, the more the court requires the ward or the ward's estate/trust to pay.

Do whatever you can always to have a few people around who have proven to be trustworthy. You're far too easily manipulated by people with psychological training when you're in a state of anxiety and confusion already. They will tell you that they're the experts. They know better. Remaining calm is always an art form. However, in this situation, it's also a survival skill.

If you're exhausted and miserable enough, there's a chance that you'll believe the people who call themselves "experts." If you fight them, they tack a description like "litigious" or "defiant" on you and make it sound like a dirty word. If you want to object to the financial reports that the commercial guardian files, if those reports have not been somehow pre-approved by the judge, I'll suggest things you can do in the Legal Matters section.

In states where expenses are pre-approved, if you want to question financial decisions, you'll have to make certain that you see proposed budgets well in advance of the judge's approval so that you can study them. If you object, say so! But do so courteously and, if possible, through a legal representative so that the 'correct' words are used, and you can't later be criticized for how you said something.

Most states make it difficult to do much to challenge a court-appointed commercial guardian or conservator. If you protest, do it on the record, even if you can't have a hearing at that time. I'll have more to say about this later.

All you can do is your best. The court usually thinks that the commercial guardian represents the court's standard of perfection. I've heard a judge insist that the commercial guardians and attorneys who routinely work in this area must not be questioned. "I know who I can trust!" he said.

Those who earn their living in the guardianship field are the experts—at least the judges think so. At best you're an ignorant lay person or a meddling relative. At worst, you're an annoyance. A fly to be shooed away, if not swatted to death.[55]

Check the law. In some states, interested parties are not allowed to contact judges directly.

Ignore their insults. Don't react. Expect these people to insult you. They have spent years learning how to irritate people the way a concert violinist learns to play a Stradivarius.

Over a period of years, people who act this way professionally often adopt the same attitude in their personal life, which means that they have probably been acting the same way at home. So, they likely treat members of their own families exactly as they're treating you.

For what it's worth, their relatives probably like their attitude just about as much as you do. A few months ago, I was having a casual conversation with a new acquaintance. When I told her what I was doing, she said, "Bet you have trouble with judges!"

"How did you know?"

"I was married to an attorney. When he was an attorney, everything was fine. Once he became a judge, he got so arrogant I had to divorce him."

At that moment, I acquired a new empathy with attorneys. Perhaps this is one reason why many legal papers are called "pleas" and "pleadings." The attorney is essentially down on bended knee, begging the judge to listen.

The safest thing for your loved one—whether that person is living in a private home or in some sort of group situation—is for one or more trustworthy people to be nearby and to visit frequently, and without needing to make appointments far in advance. That's really the only way to know what's going on.

If these visitors are interested parties in the case, everyone will need to agree with you about what's best for your loved one so you can avoid legal complications. Even if they're court-recognized interested parties, because of the current HIPAA law, they might not be able to get any reliable information about your loved one's medical condition.

What About Passing on Possessions?

What can I say about possessions? As the Rev. Billy Graham told us, long ago, a legacy of character and faith will be far more valuable to future generations than money and 'things.' So many government-created minefields can prevent all but the luckiest of families from inheriting any appreciable amounts of money or property!

Let me share with you a story about how different people's perceptions of the same items might be. In 1914, the parents of a little girl paid an itinerant artist to paint her portrait. He wasn't a famous artist, just the sort of painter who traveled around during those years, painting portraits to make a living. This painting hung, for decades, in the couple's home, where it upset the daughter every time she saw it, because it revealed that she had crossed eyes. She hated that picture all her life. The crossed eyes were corrected long before she reached adulthood.

Many years later, she inherited that portrait and hid it away in a closet. To her, it was permanent proof that she'd once had a physical problem. She didn't want to display what she perceived as her imperfection to the world.

Over the intervening years, the woman's youngest niece also saw that portrait hanging in her grandparents' home. Not knowing what it represented to the sitter, she coveted it. Finally, when the aunt was in her late eighties, the niece traveled some 2,000 miles to visit her. She demanded that her aunt give her that painting. She'd always thought it would be a great keepsake. So angry was she at her aunt's refusal that she later wrote a letter complaining that her aunt was not generous, specifically because she had refused to give her that painting.

Two different people. Two very different meanings attached to the same painting.

Speaking of giving gifts, here's a government-generated problem many families face: lookbacks (meaning audits of someone's assets going back as long as five years) allow a state to consider any major transfers of property made during that period to be examples of wrongdoing. This happens when someone is trying to qualify for long-term care under Medicaid or for other Medicaid-related services. Sometimes, even annual gifts that are allowed under federal law are not allowed under state law. All states, save one, now have a five-year lookback period.

California's lookback period is now being phased out. By 2026, it will use income as its sole determinant of whether someone is eligible for Medicaid. This makes the existing Medicaid-planning tools, including insurance trusts that attempted to shield California assets from the Medicaid lookback, obsolete. Other states often adopt laws that follow the California model. If they do so, all of those expensive work-around attempts to create trusts and other vehicles to increase elders' Medicaid eligibility will also no longer be useful.

As far as I can see, the only current way to avoid Medicaid lookback problems (everywhere except California) is to dispose of assets as you go along. And I mean many years before any suggestion of incompetence or chronic illness. Give Susie that pin she loves when she turns sixteen. Or maybe Henry gets that beloved family pocket watch when he graduates from high school. The family portrait Janie likes, well maybe you can give it to her when she moves out on her own or gets married.

If you give things away when you are at your peak of earnings and net worth, and then twenty or thirty years later something happens, you ought to be relatively safe. But only if your state doesn't change the law and the lookback period meanwhile. There are also some cases in which states consider even annual cash gifts to relatives suspect. This brings us back, once again, to the idea of consulting with a trusted accountant and/or an attorney.

The father of a friend of mine had been a billionaire. After his wife died, he began to think of his own mortality. He had both a large family and a generous nature. During the next ten years or so, my friend's father distributed most of his assets to relatives. Fifteen years later, during his own final illness, he knew his heirs would have no problems with state or federal laws. As it turned out, he was less attached to his possessions than most people might have assumed.

What does this mean? Passing on possessions must happen long before there's any thought of mental incompetence. How do we know when that's going to happen? We don't. Not really. Let's go back to the man I told you about in Chapter I, the one who had a terrible accident one day while out riding. The moment before it happened, he was fine. The next moment, he was gravely injured, unconscious, and destined to die a few days later.

Demanding that "larger" money transfers take place more than five years prior to mental incompetence or severe illness seems a lot like getting long-term care insurance with an upper monetary limit, as if you know, from the beginning, how much money you'll need, or taking 4 percent of the value of an IRA account out of that account annually, as if you already know precisely how long you'll live. Unless you're an infallible psychic, there's no way to read the future in the manner that the states and the federal government seem to expect you to.

The only sure bet in life is on uncertainty. Doctors, attorneys, accountants, and other professionals will give you a prediction based on a set of historical data and a range of possible outcomes filtered through their experience and their expertise. Usually, financial people call their prediction technique "the Monte Carlo Method." Welcome to the casino of life!

And just as the reality of uncertainty suddenly dawns on you, you also realize this: the only people you can ask for clarification—doctors, accountants, and attorneys—must report any suspected Medicare or Medicaid fraud to the state; they might lose their licenses if they don't.

Let's say a loved one has come under the control of a commercial guardian, and that ward is close to running out of money. Should that happen, it's perfectly possible for the commercial guardian to ask the court to declare that the personal property or financial assets–a portrait, corporate stock, the farm—that might have been promised to family members in the will or trust must now be sold to generate money. The court will generally comply, for reasons I'll explain in the next chapter.

If you become the legal guardian, you will be expected to ask for the same sort of court order, and the court would expect you to sell those assets prior to your loved one's death.

From what I've seen, the best time to give gifts is when your loved ones can enjoy using them, and you can bask in the good feelings generated in you by their happiness. As we know from the fairy tales most of us have heard as children, attempting to hang onto stuff often results in losing it. However, giving it away at the appropriate time and to the right person benefits both the giver and the recipient.

We've just reviewed what you might call 'voluntary giving' or 'gifting' during your lifetime. In the next chapter, I'll talk about what happens when you're grappling with the provisions of wills or trusts.

More Attempts to Maintain Control of Assets

Some attempt to safeguard family wealth by setting up limited liability companies (LLCs) or other legally created entities and placing whole-life insurance policies into them. The dividends some of these policies pay are not subject to taxes. You can also borrow against their value at a low interest rate. Then, too, the policies' values grow over time. Usually, the death benefit isn't taxable income to the beneficiaries. This wealth-protection strategy might work well in some instances.

"Insurance companies are stable," you tell yourself. "They never fail."

Wrong! In January 2019, a chart showing forty-two "major" bankruptcies of health and life insurance companies between 1914 and 2019 appeared in the industry publication *Atlas Magazine*; at least four more have been liquidated since then. "Major" meant a company that had operations in three or more states.[56] Should that happen to your or your parents' insurance company, payouts to policyholders or beneficiaries may amount to pennies on the dollar. Some states might require a top payout of under $15,000 on a life insurance policy. The rules vary from one state to the next.

Should an elder become incapacitated, however, and fail to pay back a life insurance loan, any death benefit will be diminished by that amount, plus interest. If they forgot to pay the required premiums and did not arrange to pay reduced premiums, the policy might be canceled. In addition, a court-appointed guardian might get a judge's permission to liquidate the LLC. Then there's just a stack of insurance policies listed in reports to the court among the ward's other assets. A judge might also allow the guardian to stop the payment of premiums.

Another possibility is that the court might allow these policies to be sold to a third party so that cash can be used for the elder's needs. This is known as a viatical settlement, and the estate will not be paid for the full face value. Then the policies are gone and there's no death benefit for the named beneficiaries of the original policy. The person claiming the death benefit will be the person who bought the policy (usually at a considerable discount to the face value).

I could show you more ways in which the original intention of buying insurance policies to protect beneficiaries can be frustrated, but you get the idea. These business entities and whole-life policies are only a protection, all other things being equal. The problems brought on by dementia or physical infirmity might quickly change the picture.

Refusing to follow a judge's order to sell or stop paying premiums on a policy would place the person who refused in contempt of court. Being in contempt of court might subject the guardian/conservator to fines or jail time.

Insurance trusts and insurance LLCs are not unique. For any asset the ward owns more than 50 percent of, the guardian legally has the same rights to sell or dissolve as the ward would have, provided the court approves it. The guardian might also try to dissolve other businesses in which the ward owns less than 50 percent, although the court might want to liquidate other assets first.

Conclusion

In this chapter, I've explained some of the assumptions that the courts make about the motives of elders and their families, and a little about why the authorities believe these things. As a result, guardianship reform has become complex. It involves the re-education of several professions, on a very large scale.

Sometimes, the hardest thing is to learn when it's appropriate to relinquish control for the greater good of all. I'm primarily speaking here about worldly goods. Ironically, attempting to hang onto them until the bitter end might ultimately prevent you from bequeathing them to the person you most wanted to have them, should a state-appointed guardian or the state itself step in and sell them to pay guardianship or medical bills.

TAKEAWAYS

1. The only substitute for monitoring your loved one's situation yourself is having one or more others you trust monitoring it frequently. We need to see more ethics in lawyers' and commercial guardians' billing.
2. Given that it's becoming harder to transfer property late in life, consider doing so earlier.
3. Find good legal and accounting help for everyone if you need it. Find it now. Later may be too late.
4. As hard as you might find it to dispute what "the experts" have said, find a way to register any protest. If you let a deadline for protesting slide, you might lose your rights permanently.

CHAPTER VII

What Might the Other Players Want You to Sign?

N ow, as a non-attorney, I'll take you on a brief tour of the sorts of legal documents and authorities you're likely to encounter when your loved one needs help with decision-making. My experiences are common to members of the public when dealing with them. Statutes and rules make them binding, often prescribing punishments if you don't obey them. Rules (generally adopted by licensing boards or the courts) are easier to change, because they don't require the approval of a legislature and a governor.

Laws and regulations in various states change from time to time. Many states have what they call a 'uniform probate code,' to which documents relating to estates and to the care of defenseless (incapacitated) people generally belong.

Don't be fooled by the word "uniform." The text of a 'model law' might once have been sent out by the American Bar Association, but states often change the text before enacting these laws. They now vary from state to state. So far, Louisiana still has statutes derived from French law (the Napoleonic Code) and not from English law. Other states base most of their laws on English common law. So, a great deal depends on where you live and where your loved one lives.

Next, we'll look at attorneys, judges, and other related court functionaries. Watching how they interact, members of the public sometimes wonder how any of them can truly claim neutrality. There is hope, however, as I know because I've met some attorneys who are truly open-minded. I only wish there were more of them!

In the final section of this chapter, we'll look at some of the paperwork either judges, trustees, conservators, executors, or guardians might want you to sign. People often find that they have lost far more than they gained by signing some of these documents.[57] Be sure to ask a trusted attorney to confirm what you think a document says.

Powers of Attorney, Trusts, Conservatorships, and Guardianships

According to what I've read, experienced, and heard, a person's last years are often full of painful surprises; times during which friends and family and those with legal power do not perform as expected. In 44 BC, when he was in his sixties, the Roman statesman, lawyer, and philosopher Cicero authored a short book whose title translates to *On Old Age*. What worried him? "The shifts of fortune," he wrote, "test the reliability of friends."

Our problems haven't changed all that much. And what is it that we want our friends and family and attorneys to do for us?

For one thing, everyone now seems to want those over sixty to sign a financial power of attorney. This helps if you're sick for a while, or away, and there are bills due like rent and taxes and someone must pay them. But being absent now is far less of a problem than it used to be. Wherever on Earth you are you can pay most bills online if there's internet access. And you can also set up a checking account to pay certain bills automatically every month. I suspect that some parts of the laws governing powers of attorney might already be obsolete.

A healthcare power of attorney may take effect if, for instance, you've been in an accident and are unconscious. Someone else must give the doctors consent to treat you. But how will a hospital know who has this right? Is that information readily accessible if your cell phone is locked?

Problems crop up with both of these documents. Regularly. What if you say you don't want a particular treatment used, but a new, more effective, and less unpleasant version of it has recently been developed? There's now a long list of medical procedures that used to require a six inch to foot-long incision into your abdomen but now only require a half inch-long incision.

Perhaps, when you filled out the medical power of attorney, you were only familiar with the old procedure. Seeing that procedure named on the sheet on which you'd written your instructions and a statement that you don't want it used, the person holding the power of attorney refuses the treatment on your behalf, and you either die or are permanently injured. Given the way the power of attorney was written, those were your instructions.

With financial powers of attorney, similar problems can arise. You might own property in a once-desirable area, and the area can deteriorate. If you've said that it should be held or don't give the person holding the POA the power to sell it, then the person with power of attorney can't sell it.

The history of lawsuits is filled with the names of fiduciaries who ignored clear instructions. But keeping that property, because of the declining property values in its vicinity, is going to cause the owner to lose a lot of money. Any fiduciary is required to act in the best interests of the money and property being managed. This question of which decision is correct is often resolved in court.

Your state might not require banks to accept general powers of attorney that a lawyer can make up for you in his office. They have their own forms, or they demand additional documentation. Banks are likely to report that they suspect some sort of abuse if an older person comes in and meets specific criteria they've been given that they think suggest someone might be manipulating that person into naming the other person as POA.

Another wrinkle is that they now seem to require all powers of attorney to be renewed every five years (at least). And they far prefer the account holder and the proposed holder of the power of attorney to arrive separately when the document is being drawn up. No one will tell me why, but I'm assuming that they're looking for evidence of possible dementia or coercion and they will report the account holder to state authorities if they think they've found any.

This is true for investment accounts, as well. Stockbrokers, too, have their own forms, although they don't always insist that the person go with you to the broker's office to be vetted. If they know an elder well, they might not. And for the many online brokers, in-person transactions are now all but impossible.[58]

If a trust already exists, a court almost always names a commercial trustee. The commercial trustee must be paid, and so money from the trust pays the trustee, leaving less money for the original beneficiaries.

It seems to me that the invisible playbook for guardians and conservators must counsel them to create a trust, if possible. One major reason is to set the terms of the trust themselves and to name either themselves or someone they already know will cooperate with them to be the trustee.

What's my beef with setting up a trust? Well, I know a family whose matriarch set up a family trust. She appointed her son as the trustee. The trust gave her son great powers and no oversight. She knew the future trustee very well. The son managed this money until his mother developed dementia. When a commercial guardian was appointed, the court suddenly said the son wasn't a trained money manager and there were millions of dollars in that trust. (Well, there had always been millions of dollars in it; no one had complained before.)

To be fair, the judge also realized that the son was only one of the heirs, and those heirs didn't always agree. The court wanted a "recognized expert" in charge. Instead of the woman's son, the judge appointed a mutual friend of the commercial guardian and the judge.

The new trustee, an attorney, charged his customary hourly legal fees for everything, even what looked on his invoices like clerical work. It didn't take long before all the cash was gone, and he was selling the matriarch's other holdings to pay bills. A few years later, the ward passed away and the guardianship case ended. The millions of dollars originally in the trust had dwindled to a few thousand dollars per heir.

The family had often objected to his actions, so the trustee got the judge to sign off on his actions, thereby making himself practically suit-proof. After that, he dissolved the trust and distributed its few remaining assets to the four beneficiaries.

Having even a huge but finite amount of money is no longer a guarantee of financial comfort. It all depends on cash flow and debt obligations. *Wall Street Journal* reporter Robert Frank once described the descent into bankruptcy of a billionaire.[59] It can happen, and paradoxically may surprise those who are trying the hardest to conserve family wealth.

Some parents, trying to prevent suits among their heirs, make the choice of trustee irrevocable. The sort of disaster I'm about to describe can be the ultimate result of trying to insulate heirs against disagreements.

I once heard Ric Edelman, the former financial guru of public television, speaking on the radio. A listener called in, complaining that his family's irrevocable trust had been operating for decades, ever since his parents died. The parents had named a corporate trustee who charged just about the equivalent of the trust's income annually, thereby leaving the adult children for whom the parents had wanted to provide with no income for themselves. There seemed to be no provision in the trust to allow them to oust an unsatisfactory trustee, so Ric Edelman warned them that it looked as if the heirs were stuck until there were no assets left in that trust.

Even trusts created by the most expensive attorneys in the world—the so-called 'perpetual' or 'dynastic' trusts—won't protect family mega-fortunes forever. In the nineteenth and early twentieth centuries, the Rothchild family owned a constellation of fabulous estates all over Europe (and more than one in the United States, as well).

Inheritances for almost 200 heirs cut into their wealth. Most of the Rothschild real estate is no longer in the family. In 2019, the Rothschilds sold their last property in Austria.

As for John D. Rockefeller's storied nest of trusts, consider this sobering quote from Robert Frank's 2008 *Wall Street Journal* article that assessed the continuing influence of certain members of that family: "With more than 150 living blood relatives of John D. Rockefeller Sr., many members of the latest generation of the family . . . . aren't likely to be able to live off their dwindling family trusts, according to people close to the family."[60]

Some states don't allow people to set up perpetual trusts. What I find even odder is that other states have laws limiting the number of years a perpetual trust is allowed to operate. Doesn't "perpetual" mean that it lasts forever? Apparently not anymore.

The only way I've observed that money can be passed efficiently from generation to generation is through a major foundation or a charity. That way, the younger generation works for the foundation and might receive money from the foundation in perpetuity. But you must be on the financially exalted financial level of a Bill Gates or a Warren Buffet for this to work for a few generations. Even then, it's impossible to predict how long the money will last.

Several attorneys have told me that the purpose of a trust is to be dissolved so that the remaining assets can be distributed to either the original beneficiaries or what are called "remaindermen." This second category consists of people to whom assets will be given if the original beneficiaries die. My question is: why not just distribute the assets to the right people in the first place? Some people worry that their heirs will run through their inheritance. Is the dwindling of assets, over time, that I've just described really that much of an improvement?

As most of us have read in fairy tales, attempting to keep control doesn't work well. Your plan to provide protection may backfire. People frequently create trusts because they want privacy. They don't want anyone to know what they are giving to others as an inheritance.

That secrecy comes at a price. The price is often that you can't have an open and honest discussion or that you have no control over your loved one's papers after their death (because they belong to the trust, not to you). Sometimes, it means that you can't get any information while they're alive because the trustee is allowed, by a judge, to refuse you access to them or information about them, or both.

In April 2020, the IRS announced a huge crackdown on what it called "abusive" trust schemes. Many different sorts of trusts aimed at avoiding taxes have now become its special targets.

As the former trustee of two now-dissolved trusts that were not set up to avoid taxes and never saw anyone from the IRS question any action taken, I can say this from personal experience: it might be more realistic to pay the taxes than to compensate a nest of people levying various administrative, legal, and tax preparation fees on a trust over time. In my opinion, the trust's main virtue is its secrecy. Its tax efficiency will change as the law changes.

Conservatorship (sometimes it's called "guardianship of the estate" or a similar name, depending on state law) doesn't quite give a conservator the sort of power a trust can. It normally ends at death or shortly afterward.

In New Mexico, a bill was introduced recently to allow a conservator to keep control of the ward's property for at least a year after that person passed away. If it had been enacted and signed by the governor, the ward's estate (if any) would have had to continue to pay any invoices submitted to the trust or estate of the deceased ward because the conservator would have remained as a court-appointed functionary, now officially named automatically and by law.

Any remaining money in the estate or trust might also have gone to pay the guardian for a year, even though the ward had already died. The same law might be re-introduced. Watch for a similar proposal coming soon to a legislature near you.

A similar law might well pass in other states, particularly if no one is watching. Such laws might mean that the family has little to no say in funeral arrangements and the deceased ward's conservator will stay on as the ward's executor (at least for the year following the ward's demise), regardless of what the ward's will or trust states.

Once again, make certain you examine carefully any stated preferences a mentally incapacitated person may have expressed. Where (and exactly when) did the person make these statements or write these things down? Had their competency already been questioned? Did someone else write these statements?

Wills

What can I say about wills? I've seen will contests poison relationships down through at least four generations of different families.[61] In my opinion, it might look as if someone wins and someone else loses, but in my opinion, everyone loses, and family cohesion most of all. Whether in probate or if there's a trust, the fastest way to lose money and fracture your family is to argue over it in court. There are two ways to avoid this: be honest and keep things as simple and transparent as possible.

Again, in cases where there are multiple beneficiaries and a trust, they must all agree and sign a stipulated order saying this, or the court is likely to impose a trust controlled by a trustee of the court's choosing. The heirs might not like this result at all. At the opposite extreme, I've seen more than one person refuse to go against the majority and then spend the rest of time fuming about what they were strong-armed into signing.

If you don't want to sign, don't do it. You can contest what a trustee or conservator has done, but be aware that the consequences might ultimately include everyone getting next to nothing as the trustee or conservator sits there, continuing to collect large fees and pay expensive attorneys out of a trust's or estate's assets.

It used to be expensive to change a will. However, now, with legal services offering subscriptions where you pay little or nothing to revise a will, even annually, that objection isn't valid any longer. But there are other considerations, too.

If you always try to minimize taxes, you'll end up having to change legal documents whenever the law changes. Why? Each time the public finds a tax loophole, the federal government learns about what they're doing. Then, in plugging up that loophole, the government always seems to create a new loophole. Once again, this situation parallels the old fairy tales. The more you try to avoid taxes, the more likely that they will have changed just after you made a will and that you will die after they change, leaving your heirs in a bigger tax hole than if you hadn't changed anything.

What's Fair About All of This?

Who said that life was always fair? There's no room here for an extended discussion of the seeming contradiction of calling most courts that hear adult guardianship cases and wills being probated "courts of equity."[62] To most of us who have been part of proceedings there, it seems that "equity" rarely enters the picture. Many people blame the way laws are written and the power judges have to make decisions litigants can't afford to question (given the legal fees involved). Or judges' decisions can't be challenged because of technicalities in the law or the rules.

Only a large and well-organized group of aggrieved family members can make change happen in this arena. Why?

Arrayed against each family are phalanxes of lawyers. Attorneys often write guardianship laws and rules. They lobby for the guardianship profession and for other attorneys in the profession. They are salted all through the process, as you've already seen:

1. They appear as "guardians ad litem" whose function is supposed to be to protect the person whose competency is being challenged.
2. They represent both sides—whoever is doing the challenging of someone's competency and the prospective ward. If other family members are involved, those family members almost always have at least one attorney representing them, at least at the beginning.
3. They sit on the bench, acting as judges.
4. Other attorneys serve as the special masters.
5. Most of the time, they are the mediators; many retired judges serve in this capacity.
6. At times, someone trained as an attorney but no longer able to practice law becomes an employee of a guardianship firm, with legal authority over wards.

Guardians and conservators want to be absolved of any liability for what they've done in carrying out what they say are their court-appointed functions. I've already mentioned this. But freedom from oversight shouldn't extend to concealing frank wrongdoing.

Two guardianship and trust firms in New Mexico—Desert State and Ayudando—that dealt primarily with relatively small amounts of money (in this context, that means less than $500,000 per trust, for the trust firm and under $50,000 for the guardianship firm) had hundreds of clients between them. Their total embezzlement from those people exceeded $15 million. Both firms were caught by the FBI through informants during the mid-2010s.

Most likely, their crimes would have been found out far sooner had the veil of secrecy over guardianship cases in New Mexico been lifted. They had the protection of that secrecy to cloak all their actions, and the absence of effective audits that had the power to ask for indictments. Without the whistle-blowers who exposed their wrongdoing to the feds, they'd likely still be fleecing the helpless.

After the guardianship scandals of 2017, when their crimes were publicized, the New Mexico courts listed adult incompetence cases on the court agenda, just like all other cases. Divorce, bankruptcy, the probate of wills, and bad credit suits have never been secret processes. Why all the secrecy around adult guardianship? During the next few years, it looked as if the system was becoming more transparent.

Eventually, however, the press attention subsided. Then, the courts reverted to secrecy. The name of the potential ward, the court-appointed experts, the guardian, even most of the attorneys once again disappeared from public view; not only from the daily court agendas, but also the dockets themselves avoided mention of the players, often simply stating, "guardian appointed."

As I'm writing this, you'll see on the New Mexico court agendas scheduled hearings involving name changes, people being sued for nonpayment of debt, accident cases, and many other situations some people might find embarrassing. The schedule publishes the names of all involved. There's only one category—adult guardianship—in which all the names of the potential wards, defendants, plaintiffs, and interested parties and their attorneys are once again blocked out on the court agendas so you can't see them. (Even divorce and child custody at least mention some of the players.)

All that shows in adult guardianship cases, however, is the name of the judge, the name of one attorney, and the fact that it's a guardianship case. To me, this looks like unequal treatment in one sort of case.

Honorable guardians, conservators, and trustees have no reason to fear public scrutiny. Their very honesty protects them as they give careful and accurate accountings and tell the court the truth.

What do untrustworthy guardians and conservators and trustees want?

1. You should never say anything bad about them or their profession, which might cut into their reputation and earning power.
2. To limit your access to the ward, to information, and to documents.
3. To be immune from both public and private criticism, and to be protected from lawsuits.

My own experience leads me to believe that they would really prefer that the relatives of their wards stay in the shadows and never speak in public again.

By the time a judge's unilateral gag order cut off a large part of my freedom of speech and put severe social limits on me, I'd met other people laboring under various sorts of gag orders in guardianship cases. Some of their relatives had already died. I could see how they kept looking around corners, afraid someone might report them for some imagined infraction and get them fined for contempt. In the next-to-last chapter, I'll talk more about how some people can get such gag orders lifted, as I eventually did.

Not all judges are receptive to guardians requesting gag orders. A few years ago, a judge in New York refused to impose such an order, stating that it didn't affect the ward one way or another. Instead, it benefited only the commercial guardian while harming the family through the denial of their freedom of speech. Bravo! However, he was an exception. We need to find more such jurists.

Only a judge can say, "I'm writing the order; you, Jane's son, are her guardian now. The commercial guardian is out of the picture."

No one else has that authority. Many commercial guardians have told family members they're willing to step aside and not "object" to that family member taking over. The family member looks at the absolute authority the guardian appears to have over their loved one and assumes this means, "They're giving me the guardianship! Wow! I've won!"

Not so fast!

If anyone else in the case objects, the 'deal' is almost certainly off. That one person might not even be a family member. It might be the guardian ad litem or the special master or a psychologist. The commercial guardian will probably have a good idea which person is going to object, even before that firm makes you the offer to step aside. Suppose the incapacitated person started out with a commercial guardian. In that case, it's almost certain that, if the current commercial guardian dies or resigns from the case, unless there's a spate of adverse publicity, the judge will appoint another commercial guardian.

I've only known of a few recent cases where a relative took over after having worked for years to get the judge to agree. They almost always involved some press or community intervention, or both.

Even when dealing with families that have no money, the court often gives the guardianship of their incapacitated members to commercial firms.[63]

Let's say your state requires the guardian to present a report listing their ward's already-paid expenses. Let's also say you're living in a state where you're what's called an "interested party;" you're supposed to get a copy. (In some states this information is still not released to anyone.) Once the judge formally approves a guardian's annual reports, you won't have any recourse later. To preserve your rights, you must object as close to immediately as possible.

Be certain that your attorney has **written** instructions from you not to sign these reports as approved on your behalf until you've had time to look them over and comment in writing. Find out whether there is a specific length of time during which the court allows you to file an objection. Have those rules changed since the last annual report?

As I've already warned you, in some states, you are not allowed to write anything directly to the judge, so be careful to check the current requirements in your state first. If your attorney does something you've clearly instructed them not to do, having filed written instructions not to sign off automatically on the guardians' reports might give you some legal protection.

Many family members complain that trustees, guardians, and conservators use the ward's money to fight them in court. As you saw earlier in this chapter, so do executors and trustees. All the attorneys I've consulted say this is customary and established practice. I've written and spoken about this in detail elsewhere, but right now there's not much we can do to prevent them from doing this.

For as long as the ward lives, dishonest or power-hungry guardians and conservators will try to withhold as much information as they can from others concerned about the ward's welfare. They can do this by saying they're protecting the ward's privacy. Having a case in probate court might allow the release of documents that a case held as part of a guardianship or trust proceeding will not.

Normally, any commercial entity administering an estate will advise the heirs to make as little trouble for the establishment as possible. The more complaining they do, the higher the legal fees and the less inheritance they receive. If what you primarily care about is money, that's true. It cost me more than ten times as much in court-related fees after Mama died than it had before. However, I'd say that less than ten percent of that cost came from the probate case itself, but rather from the documents (there were more than 40,000 altogether) I managed to get by having my attorney send subpoenas to the right people during the probate case. These offered a large part of the information I needed to sue my mother's guardian.

To know what happened to your loved one, you'll need to see what people wrote during the guardianship/conservatorship. In recent years, most health workers have computerized their records. In that process, they adopted a 'check-the-boxes' form of reporting rather than creating short essays to describe their meetings with patients. This is true of doctors, nurses, and health aides, as well.

This sort of record-keeping is easy to feed into a scanner and computerize. Or it can be done on a laptop or cell phone from the beginning. But it's also a good way to avoid providing detailed information on a particular meeting or event.

There's an axiom in health care that if it's not in the written or digital record it didn't happen. Because they see so many patients, everyone involved in caring for a patient used to make note of anything distinctive that happened to help them remember the event. Now they don't want to remember. It's a good bet that most won't recall an unusual event if subpoenaed.

This provides what politicians call "plausible deniability." If called to the witness stand, they can honestly say, "I cared for a thousand patients that month, Mr. Smith. I can't recall whether that happened to this specific patient or not. It's not in the record."

If you can get and read the documents, either they will tend to confirm your suspicions or they will show you that no one did anything wrong. One of the nice things (at least from my perspective) that is still true in finance is that all conversations about investments a broker or brokerage house has with someone tend to be memorialized and sent to the back office. The back office keeps them for at least five years.

Banks have their own policies. The length of time institutions must keep documents may vary depending on changes in state and federal requirements. However, at this point, financial records (and particularly in-house notes on financial conferences, if you have questions about how your loved one's money was managed) might give you more detailed information than more recent health records that are computerized.

Either way, this information will help you decide the best way to go in the future. You might just have closure as you discover that you have already done all you could. You no longer must wonder and feel guilty. Guilt retained can fester and ruin your life. Anyone who cared about you would not want you to live that way.

The takeaway from this would be: Don't ever make large purchases or take out loans on the assumption that any inheritance you've been promised will get to you intact. And that's particularly true if heavy health expenses for your loved one, in addition to commercial guardian and conservator firms, are involved.

It may be that commercial guardians are really trying to protect themselves against you by being so secretive, although they claim to be protecting the ward's privacy. Again, it's like living in one of those horrible fairy tales where the more you try to avoid something, the more it pursues you.

The commercial guardians whose actions I'm familiar with tend to hide every scrap of information they can and only to make statements that relatives might find misleading. This always seems to drive the family members of their wards into a frenzy of anxiety about what they're not being told.

The daughter of one ward was horrified to hear her mother's guardian casually remark that, although her mother was in the hospital, she wasn't dying "at the moment." They wouldn't allow the daughter to visit her mother or call her on the phone. They even refused to tell her which hospital her mother was in or what her problem was. That confusing statement really upset her. It also led her to ask whether the guardian considered the ward's death to be coming soon.

Check your state's rules and laws (and those of the state your loved one lives in) and don't sign anything you don't have to. This is where you need to find an honorable attorney to explain to you, in detail, the meaning of what you've signed (or are considering signing), and whether changes in the situation—as I'll explain in Chapter IX—might make a court modify or lift these restrictions.

Even though that's a conflict of interest, I've seen some unscrupulous lawyers claim to be working simultaneously for both the guardian (or the ward) and for another interested party, with results that are routinely bad for the family of the ward. As I was writing this section, a friend of mine called to report yet another instance of this happening.

If your state's court dockets are published, one way to do a superficial check of this is to query the guardian's name and see whether the attorney you're considering using is also listed on those dockets as representing the same guardianship or conservatorship firm in another case. (As I've already mentioned, some court systems have adopted a system of disguising this association by no longer naming the guardian who has been appointed by simply stating "guardian appointed" or something similar. Since dockets are singularly confusing to lay people anyway, this sort of research can only be a hit-or-miss effort.)

Even if the legal firm doesn't have a record of representing the guardianship firm, someone else might. Or they might say that they do.

We'll discuss the judges in more detail than before in the next section.

Judges

In this section, I'll give you a quick overview of the range of behaviors you can expect, should you ever have to deal with a person in black robes who sits on a court bench. "Judges," legal scholar and media personality Alan Dershowitz says, "are the weakest link in our judicial system, and they are also the most protected."[64]

One judge I follow has given multiple media interviews discussing adult guardianship. He always says it's the family's fault if a relative is in a commercial guardianship situation. Any pain the relatives experience, he always says, is only what they deserve.

Why do they deserve punishment? According to him, that relative has been placed under the care of a commercial entity only because the family is dysfunctional in some way. And yes, I know that I've said this before. However, frequently reminding yourself of it might just save your sanity. All the evidence I've seen and heard confirms this is the prevailing belief in 'professional' circles. The guardianship profession believes this. Many judges believe this. Most attorneys believe this. They've been taught this belief in school.

I've spoken with only one attorney who categorically denies ever having heard in law school that families are hotbeds of conflicting interests, and that their members are naturally always in competition. While I accept what she says about her experience, I've spoken with others who attended the same law school she did. They confirmed to me that they heard this from their professors. My guess is either that she missed that day's lecture, or that she was temporarily distracted when her teacher taught this theory.

Apparently, almost the entire legal profession's bad opinion of family members also extends to the family members of those injured and mentally challenged individuals I mentioned previously. The New Mexico court required someone other than their families to set up and administer trusts for them. Then those same guardians and conservators stole the Social Security payments, VA pensions, and accident settlement funds out of those trusts.

The judges had initially insisted that the families couldn't manage that money. That's why they arbitrarily appointed professionals to do the job. In effect, the judge was saying to the family, "This settlement you've won in court for your loved one is for more money than you've ever had, so I don't trust you to handle it honestly or competently. I don't even trust you to learn how to handle it. I'm going to use the power the state vested in me to give that money to someone else to manage, someone I trust."

I feel safe in saying that no family is perfect. Not even that judge's family. The same judge who's casting all those stones. Might the members want to learn? Does he truly believe that the members can't learn?

In the interests of full disclosure, my take on this is that all members of the medico-legal system are indoctrinated to be prejudiced against family members. This bias against the family members of people who can't make decisions independently crosses class lines, ethnic lines, racial lines, gender lines—in fact it oppresses all parts of society. If you are a family member or significant other of someone in need of guardianship, you likely have a bullseye on your back. You just might not know it yet.

Often the "My calendar's so crowded!" complaint from a judge who says he's overwhelmed by the volume of cases he must deal with is followed by an appeal for more staff and a bigger budget. But the budget and the staff won't help unless everyone is willing to come out and say whatever they have to say about guardianship cases in a public hearing that results in a public transcript. Most aren't.

Most jurists wouldn't go on the public record and say those horrid things about families in their own courtroom. To do so would subject their decisions to censure, because the judge would have expressed prejudice against one side of the legal case. It's a public statement that increases the likelihood that these decisions might be overturned on appeal. Yet they feel perfectly well justified in generating publicity designed to shame and demonize the family members of wards.

I've heard all the stories of cronyism, too. The judges who were the gym buddies of the counsel for the guardian (or perhaps even the commercial guardian). Judges who went on shopping sprees with people on the guardian's side of the case. A friend once told me of going to a rural courtroom for a hearing. When the hearing adjourned for the morning, the judge, and the lawyers for both sides turned out to be related, and they all went to lunch together.

Did those rural lawyers (the judge was a lawyer, too) do something incredibly corrupt? It sure does look bad! But then, maybe they were the only lawyers in that small town, and they were just sitting there at lunch, gossiping about their family members. If you live in a larger urban center, this relatedness and the cronyism issue might pose less of a problem. Or they might be more of a problem but more easily hidden.

A word about judicial standards. Years ago, I heard a radio broadcast. The man being interviewed headed a New Mexico group called the Judicial Standards Commission. He made an impressive presentation about how they rate judges and are fair and non-partisan. Then, they recommend to the public whether the judge should be retained in the next election. "Sounds great!" I thought to myself. Then they broke for an announcement.

What was the next thing out of the mouth of the man who ran the Commission? "Of course," he said, "we never accept complaints from the public. We know that we're only going to hear from malcontents who don't like the judge's decision. Someone who wins isn't going to complain. So, we only listen to attorneys and judicial colleagues and court personnel. They're the only ones who know."

Again, as with the 8.5 million websites complaining about guardianship abuses, couldn't even a percentage of complaints from members of the public have merit? Even as few as ten similar complaints out of one hundred might signal a systemic problem any standards commissions ought to want to solve.

I know members of the public who complained about judges and about cases in which their families were then involved and never heard back from the State Commission. North Carolina and Montana also have commissions that are supposed to oversee judges. Tennessee calls it The Board of Judicial Conduct. If your state has a similar group that evaluates judges, check its policies toward the public carefully before sending in any complaints.

If you are waiting for help and your state has a policy of not listening to members of the public, you might more profitably spend your time on some other activity. Or find a way to change the commission's policies before you complain.

Most likely, these 'judicial standards' commissions are not even seeing the tip of the iceberg of cases of judicial misconduct, even those from lawyers. I've heard more than one attorney complain to me that his state judicial ethics commission, regardless of what it's called, keeps careful track of which annual questionnaire belongs to which attorney.

If the questionnaire is not sent back, these attorneys say, they get repeated calls to their office. What does the clerk say? "You didn't send in your judge evaluations this year."

They interpret this as evidence that their responses are being care-fully tracked and tied to their names, and that any negative evaluations might result in reprisals. Do you think that this absolute lack of privacy in the voting booth (so to speak) encourages attorneys to rush to speak their mind if they truly want to complain about questionable judicial actions? Or do the commissions tend to disallow all complaints, assuming it's sour grapes because an attorney lost a specific case?

One attorney did try to challenge a judge for misconduct. He was representing someone in a case that was on appeal. This judge had recently been appointed to the appeals court and was presiding over that case. However, she had judged the same case in a lower court for five years before the appeal was filed.

If she stayed on that appeals case as the judge, she would be ruling on the same case twice. Wasn't this some sort of conflict of interest? How many judges are likely to say, "Whoops! I goofed last time; this time around, I'm going to do a better job?"

To prove his case, the attorney needed transcripts from a sequestered guardianship case that he'd worked on, the one she'd been judging in the lower court. The judge, now sitting on the appeals court, my source told me, refused him the right to use them on the grounds that those records were sequestered and should not be used. This judge stayed on the case, ruled against the attorney's client, and he was soon disbarred. Is it any wonder that charges of judicial corruption and improper judicial action are so rare? And again, denial that this sort of thing is happening does a bad situation no good.

Judges get 'guardianized' too. Perhaps the most egregious example of this is the case of Judge John Phillips of Brooklyn, New York, a jurist who started out with assets including $20 million in real estate. After he began exhibiting symptoms of dementia, another judge appointed a commercial guardian who took over Judge Phillips's life. The succession of court-appointed guardians sold almost everything their ward owned. Most of what wasn't sold burned up in a fire caused by the guardian's lack of maintenance and dropping a building's fire insurance.

According to the *New York Times*, he froze to death in a nursing home in 2008.[65]

Judges are taught that family members are manipulative and self-interested. They later get this same information from attorneys and organizations whose membership consists of commercial guardians and conservators who have an interest in staying in business. They're indoctrinated to believe that the industry has the defenseless person's interests foremost in their thoughts, protecting them from the predations of relatives. You're unlikely to be able to reeducate jurists by yourself, but I'll discuss more options in Chapter X.

What do you do now? Find an honest attorney. A hint: a guardian in business for some time is likely to have already consulted with one attorney from all the largest law firms around, so you can save time by starting your search with smaller ones. Might this put you at a disadvantage? Maybe, but it will also get you answers faster.[66]

Paradoxically, as slowly as court cases seem to the public to creep along, things are often happening behind the scenes when you don't see anything written on the court dockets. Most attorneys do far more negotiating than litigating. Guardianship and probate are civil matters, and some 95 percent of such cases are settled before trial. As you'll see later, some authorities say the percentage is even higher than this. Standard legal opinion is that settlements tend to favor the plaintiffs because the defendants just want the suit to go away.[67] You also need that time so your lawyer can prepare.

Sometimes, too, like when someone in control is withholding food and water or medical care from a ward, it's an emergency. A call to Life Legal Defense Foundation might be on the agenda.[68]

Make sure your attorney isn't afraid to speak up on your behalf, and always have a litigator in reserve ready to jump in if needed; preferably an expert litigator who is willing to take on a guardianship case and who is not a member of the guardianship attorneys' inner circle. You need someone who can think independently, not someone who is likely to go along to get along.

To emphasize this again: Make certain to file any objections as the court requires—whether you're allowed to do it yourself or the court requires that you have an attorney do it. And make sure this happens within the time limits the court specifies.

Do you wonder whether your attorney will remember to show you any reports prior to accepting them on your behalf? Do make sure there's a paper trail stating that this is your standing request. If you plan to take on this sort of action, and what you see (on the advice of your attorney) is bad enough, be prepared to request a formal hearing in front of a jury or to have your attorney engage a forensic accountant who is willing to testify, should that become necessary. Either you or your loved one's estate will pay (a lot) for this service.

A judge denying you a trial with a jury appears to be denying you a constitutional right. That fact alone might provide you with an additional reason to sue. But remember, too, that appeals take time and cost money.

Making a laundry list of a thousand complaints, large and small, and then throwing them all up against a wall to see what sticks might backfire badly. The other side can frustrate you by making every attempt to paint you as frivolous or just plain nasty if you do that. Don't give them ammunition to use against you. Pick your causes carefully.

Juries often make miscreants nervous. The judge and the other side will quickly realize that, even if they manage to place a gag order on you, it's unlikely that they'll be able to keep six or twelve people (depending on the size of the jury) quiet forever. At some point, your dissatisfaction will be known to reporters who cover the court beat in your area; it's their business to find and report on unexpected events. More about this in Chapter X.

At this point, the painful truth becomes a source of power for you. Time is on your side now. The longer the disagreement drags on without a resolution, the more likely that your loved one will not survive. And if your loved one doesn't survive until the time that a hearing is scheduled, it's less likely that the guardian/conservator can get a 'final report' automatically approved, which means you will still have some legal wiggle-room.

If your loved one owns assets outside of a trust, you will have a good argument to go into probate court instead of keeping these discussions and hearings inside of a sequestered guardianship case. Check on what sorts of property can allow you to file a case in probate court, where all proceedings are public, by default. If you are very lucky, your loved one will have named you as personal representative or executor. I'll explain this more later. If there's a trust and the ward has passed away, you might need to sue the trustee.

Most wards don't survive under commercial guardianship for more than four years. I was once told three, but that was back in 2003. Perhaps wards are stronger now or conditions have improved

Families of wards who attempt to act *pro se* (as their own attorneys) almost always fail. I know of only one who succeeded handily while the ward was still alive. For anyone else who seemed to have won, it turned out to be a pyrrhic victory.

My friend who won quickly was not an attorney, but she was the daughter of a distinguished civil rights attorney and had spent time working in his law office. As long as you stay as calm as you can, find an honest attorney, and pay close attention to your attorney's instructions, as well as to the deadlines and requirements of your state courts, you'll have a far better chance of coming out of this process in one piece.

In the next section, we'll discuss the various legal papers the guardian, conservator, trustee, and their attorneys might want you to sign.

What Did They/Can They Make You Sign?

By now, you're familiar with powers of attorney, and you know quite a bit about how they work, so I'm not going to spend a lot of time on them here.

Right now, I'm going to concentrate on the paperwork involved in petitioning the court to set up a guardianship or conservatorship. Then I'll discuss the various reports you might be asked to approve. In between, there are often "stipulated orders" and other orders issued by the judge that generally represent the resolution of some sort of dispute.

Once again: read everything carefully, and with the help of a good attorney, before you sign. In my opinion, that's money well spent. You need to know—as thoroughly as humanly possible—what you are agreeing to do (or not do). Words matter. And here, that means the way those words would be interpreted in a court of law, not the way a member of the public would read them. No one should be able to 'make' you sign something your attorney says will harm you.

"Inertia, incompetence, status, power, cost, and risk are a formidable set of motivations to keep legalese . . . . These motivations lack any intellectually or socially acceptable rationale; they amount to assertions of naked self-interest." So wrote the late Prof. Robert W. Benson of Loyola Law School.

Understand that, in our adversarial legal system, if the people arrayed against you want you to sign something, they didn't write the document for your benefit. Your default assumption should be that it's been written expressly for the joint purposes of increasing their power over you and minimizing their risk.

If something goes seriously wrong either in the guardianship or between the commercial guardian and the family of the ward—or if the commercial guardian firm thinks it might—they might want to attempt to ensure their legal release from any liability. They'll do this by asking you to sign a waiver of one sort or another. A simple release from liability would be one way. A non-disparagement agreement (to prevent you from ever saying anything negative about them) would be another.

A third sort of control a guardian might try to exercise over the family of a ward would be a document, signed by a judge, commanding you either not to associate with certain people or not to give out any information relating to the ward. This comes from the judge, and you often don't have any choice or even a hearing before it's imposed. I've been told that this happens with some frequency. I know others who have experienced this sort of thing, and it happened to me.

During the period when the New Mexico guardianship dockets were open and searchable online, I noticed that about 40 percent of those cases had some sort of protective (secrecy) order in the court's files. Non-disclosure and Non-disparagement agreements would normally be made with the ward's guardian and would not find their way into the court record.

I've even spoken with people who had orders in their loved one's guardianship cases that they never saw, because their attorney never gave them copies. One person told me there was one in her relative's case that forbade the entire family of a ward from engaging a specific attorney.

Back to the origin of a guardianship proceeding. Someone is supposed to sign the initial 'complaint' that starts it. I've seen a judge allow an unsigned complaint to open up a case that resulted in him ordering the imposition of an emergency guardianship. Theoretically, that cannot happen, but it did in that instance.

I believe Florida was the first state to allow anyone to start the legal process leading to guardianship. The generic term for a similar law, enacted in a different state, is still the "Baker Act."

Any competent person of legal age can go to a circuit court in Florida and swear that another person is either a danger to him/herself or to others. This idea spread to many other states after that. I used to know an attorney who had practiced for years in Florida. He told me that a great many people were unfairly taken out of society by greedy relatives or neighbors or so-called friends in this manner. They were grabbed from their homes, he told me, taken to mental institutions for a day or two, and then drugged just before they were required to take the mental status exam mandated by the Baker Act.

The public was told that enacting these sorts of laws would protect them against possible mass shooters by allowing anyone to report any suspicious actions. This does not seem to have been true in practice, or all the mass shootings we've seen during the past decade would not have happened. However, these laws seem to have carried off into permanent guardianship quite a few sane seniors.[69]

It's easier for states to sentence elders to this sort of confinement in the context of an 'administrative' procedure rather than a full hearing in a court of law. Families are currently complaining that the requirements of a civil proceeding are far less stringent than a case in criminal law. Administrative law demands even less proof than civil court proceedings.

Complaints against current procedures include the following: 'Witnesses' often appear only in the form of letters or reports during administrative law hearings and often during civil proceedings. This makes it impossible to cross-examine anyone. Almost always, in cases like these, there is some sort of state-appointed guardian who is not a family member. Either that person is appointed in district court, or the guardian is named at one of the administrative hearings I just mentioned by an administrative law judge. From the cases I've seen, the guardian appointed is almost never a family member and never met the person before.

Administrative hearings in almost any field take place in secret. Think about a problematic school administrator or teacher who has not committed a crime. Chances are that the school board insists they can't comment on what's happening. Often, even after it's all over, they will still tell the public that it was an "administrative proceeding" and therefore confidential.

Here's how this works, in practice. I volunteered to do a friend a favor by looking up the case against a social worker who had had her license suspended by her state board during a proceeding in civil court. A friend of mine wanted to see the transcript of the hearing. The court informed everyone who inquired about this matter (including me) that, as an administrative matter, that proceeding would always remain secret unless the by-then-former social worker agreed to make it public. In other words, you'd need her permission to find out what she'd done that was so wrong that she'd lost her license.

When I told my friend the answer I'd gotten, she whooped, "Why would she give *anyone* permission? What sort of nonsense is that?"

You shouldn't be surprised to hear that the ex-social worker didn't give anyone this permission.

Things kept secret seem bad, wrong, or somehow inferior. When we treat people with dementia as if they need to be hidden away, as if no one should know about them and their issues, it makes their problems seem shameful. We should all remember that this is exactly how people with physical challenges used to be treated. We changed that situation and started protecting people with physical challenges. When will we do the same for dementia?

The Milken Institute's Center for the Future of Aging issued position papers and reports.[70] Their point, which is the same as mine, is that people with dementia should not have to hide away. Their problems shouldn't be kept secret. And (in my opinion and theirs) people with dementia shouldn't be kept isolated, either.

Let's say that your loved one has not been able to pass the various mental tests administered by one or more experts, in accordance with state law. A judge decrees that their mental incompetence requires a guardianship (and/or conservatorship). If you and the other heirs cannot agree on one or more of you handling this job, the judge will appoint a professional. Even if you are willing, and the heirs agree, if your loved one for any reason doesn't want a guardian or conservator, and the experts say one is needed, the court will appoint one anyway. The judge signs that order. You don't.

If you are appointed, you will likely have to sign a document accepting that duty.

In my opinion, the only time commercial guardians will say they have no objection to a family member taking over is when they believe the ward either has almost no money left or is near death, and they want you to sign a non-disparagement agreement in exchange. Even if there's no money, you might have no more than a whisper of a prayer of becoming your loved one's guardian anyway.

No matter what you think they're offering you, keep reminding yourself that the guardianship is not bestowed on you by the commercial guardian. They can promise that they won't object to you taking over. As I've already said, this doesn't mean the court-appointed experts—psychologist, guardian ad litem, or doctor won't object. Beware of 'offers' from the commercial guardian. There are almost certainly strings attached. As you debate whether to agree, make sure you'll be able to live with all the legalese in the fine print.

One attorney who shall remain nameless once told me that I'd never be able to get my own mother's guardianship back because she still had some money. I never did.

If your state allows you to communicate directly with the judge without penalty, be careful! This freedom to speak your mind might harm you. Many words have one meaning to the general public and another to the legal profession (including judges). It might benefit you more to have a lawyer review what you've written before you send it, or even write your letter. Think the matter over fifty-five times before taking a chance on the judge misunderstanding what you're saying.

If you want to object to what is being spent, object to that. Don't comment on the manners and morals of the guardian or conservator.

If the guardian has carried through in control of your loved one the entire time, and your loved one has passed away, the first thing the guardian will likely want is to administer the estate. I've looked at a number of court dockets in sequestered cases where guardians have gotten waivers from relatives of their deceased ward and then taken over as personal representative or executor of the estate.

Let's say that the ward has named a professional trust company to administer the estate. Often, the existing guardian or trustee or conservator simply gets the same sort of waiver from that entity and winds up as the personal representative (or what some states call "executor"), or the trustee named by the judge continues to act as the trustee until that trust is dissolved.

What follows is an example based on information Ric Edelman discussed in a radio show I heard on December 5, 2020.[71]

Commercial guardians have very good financial reasons to want to become executors or trustees. Like attorneys, they generally charge by the hour. If your loved one had, let's say, an estate of $1,000,000 (and that would be for everything the deceased ward owned, including life insurance), current estimates are that it would take 630 hours and a period of eighteen months for the estate to settle. I can't get good figures for trusts, but I'm assuming the figures would be similar for similar-sized trusts.

I know of one commercial guardianship firm that, in 2012, was charging $120/hour for what that company described as "after-death services." Using the figures quoted just now would have meant an income of $75,600 for the guardian over about a year and a half for administering a single million-dollar estate. This firm 'watched over' about fifty wards annually.

Providing each ward had a million-dollar estate and it administered all their estates, it would have earned $3.78 million just for exercising this function. With inflation, that $3.78 million has grown to just over $5.18 million in 2024. But many of their wards had far more assets, so they'd have earned much more.

That $120 hourly fee, counting inflation, would have risen to $163/hour in 2024. So, the guardianship firm's total fee for administering the same million-dollar estate would have risen to $102,694. And if you multiply that by fifty, the company's income for administering those estates would have risen to $5,134,700. The time needed, Ric Edelman estimated, would amount to about nine hours per week per estate. If the conservator is an attorney who regularly charges $360/hour, you can almost triple that amount.

But wait! Once a conservatorship is declared, the conservator begins a process called "marshalling the assets." It means that all the assets are identified, and they are all then retitled into the name of the guardianship, conservatorship, or trust. All that should be necessary, then, is a transfer of title to the estate, or perhaps a change of trustee. If someone dies and doesn't have a conservator, this process only starts after death. The conservator charges you for this 'marshalling' process if they charge hourly fees.

You can estimate that, for any conservatorship that has lasted a year or more, your loved one has already been paying for this process, and it has been telescoped into the time of just about a year. If an attorney gets involved, you can assume that the hourly fee for those services will be at least double what you would pay the guardian. Maybe more.[72] You will need to check the law in the state where your loved one passed on for the most recent laws and regulations.

As I've already said, in New Mexico, commercial guardians recently introduced a bill to remain in control of the estate for at least a year after the ward dies. They wanted to control both the financial and the medical records. Why would they want to do that? Follow the money. This is a potentially unlimited insurance policy the guardian and conservator can get without paying a premium to an insurance company. By having a law like this, the state is giving it to them for free. Unless, that is, you count the cost of lobbying to get legislators and the governor to support this sort of legislation.

Why on Earth would I say a thing like that? Here's why: Not only do the guardians continue to get paid by the hour (which means a conservator must remain in place to pay them, and that conservator must also be paid by the hour), but you also need to consider something you might have heard about before in other legal cases. It's called the "statute of limitations." In New Mexico, you have one year to sue the guardian after a person dies. Not after the guardian releases the records, but after the ward passes on.

The guardian would normally release these records to the personal representative or executor. But what they really want is to release the records to themselves, and then run out the statute of limitations.

Otherwise, if they'd done anything wrong during the guardianship or conservatorship, they would be required to act as an executor who suspects someone harmed the person who just died and sue the entity who committed the wrongdoing. But that would be the same guardian who is now the executor.

How many people or businesses have you ever heard of who have sued themselves? By the time they are ready to turn the matter over to the executor named in someone's will, the statute of limitations will have run out, making any suits against them impossible.

I won't detail here other reasons why any delay in getting access to the documents is harmful to the heirs and helpful to any guardian, conservator, or trustee who might wish to conceal wrongdoing. Many people have told me that my positive personal experiences with probate over a period of more than sixty years are not typical. However, I was extremely lucky to have honest attorneys and probate judges, and to have had honest and transparent executors (when I wasn't the executrix or personal representative myself).

The six wills with which I was involved went through probate relatively quickly. However, all of them involved the services of attorneys each executor respected. I never heard anyone complain about legal fees, nor did I feel like complaining about an attorney who got the job done efficiently and with as little fuss as possible. This reminds me, again, of the story from Chapter I of the engineering consultant who was urgently called in to fix a multi-million-dollar machine when no one could figure out why it stopped working.

A related question: Would you rather have the best brain surgeon you can find, or the cheapest?

Do legislators, as a group, have the same bad opinion of families as most judges? I once listened to a legislative hearing on a bill to reform the probate law. Some people want to ensure that a particular piece of property (generally real estate) goes to a specific person when they die, so they create what's called a "due on death" deed. The proposed new bill's wording would specifically allow guardians to retitle any "due on death" real estate into the regular assets of the ward's estate. Ultimately, the bill passed.

The legislator speaking to New Mexico's powerful Senate Judiciary Committee on that occasion was himself an attorney. He told stories about what he described as "greedy relatives, who might well have exercised undue influence to get those deeds in the first place, standing around, waiting for their relative to die so they can rush down to the county clerk's office and retitle property before anyone files for probate."

If you think that a relative now under guardianship will be passing any real estate to you under a "due on death deed" arrangement, recheck to see whether a similar law has been passed in your loved one's jurisdiction. Otherwise, you might be in for an unpleasant surprise later.

Since commercial guardians are 'professionals,' they are treated with deference by trust companies and banks. I saw multiple instances when the bank or trust company originally named in a ward's will to administer the estate and/or trust resigned in favor of a commercial guardian or the trust company or attorney serving as a conservator.

What does this mean? That there will never be any effective oversight of what was done during the conservatorship unless an heir is able to start some sort of audit process prior to the ward's demise, or if at least some objections are in the court record. If you let things pass over a period of years, providing you had access to the financial and social/ medical reports filed by the guardian and conservator, it will look as if you had no objections to them when they were filed.

If the time needed between the passing of the person who created the trust and the distribution of its assets is about the same for trusts and takes about as long as for estates, a $5 million trust would take 1,200 hours and forty-two months, on average, before the trustee distributes its assets. If an attorney manages a trust, let's say his hourly rate (and this is probably on the low side) is $320/hour in 2024. That means a fee of $384,000 to that attorney over the course of a year. But the heirs won't get their money for five years. The more heirs, the more time this process requires. The more time, the greater the expense.

Without including the fees of accountants or real estate agents, you can see that about 6 percent of the total value of the $5 million estate or trust (and about 8.5 percent of the million-dollar one) will be going to the attorney, conservator, or guardian. Either it is dispensed during the ward's life to marshal the person's assets, or it is paid out after they die. And sometimes, it seems to me, that fee is paid twice (even though I don't think that it should be).

Suppose all the assets are already properly titled while the ward is living under guardianship or conservatorship. Why in this age of electronic funds transfers should it take a year or more to find the right heirs and transfer those assets after the ward passes away? This is even more true given that the names and contact information of all the interested parties (they would also normally have been the heirs, too) are already known to the court and to the guardian?

A personal confession: it once took me over three months (and about ten hours of filling in forms and time spent on the phone) to accomplish an electronic transfer of a few thousand dollars' worth of stock from an account then held at a public corporation's transfer agent to an account with the same name at a brokerage house.

The transfer agent kept saying that I needed to change the form in various ways until I'd filled out a new form six times, using every possible permutation of information. Then, they finally transferred that stock. If I'd been an estate attorney, the billing on that transaction (even if my paralegal did the work) would likely have exceeded the value of the original asset by at least 50 percent.

As I write this, there's no tax on passing to family members the assets in a $5 million trust. At some point in the future, there might be.

Many people told me they had to sign releases before the commercial guardian would distribute any inheritances. I don't recall ever signing any. On the other hand, unscrupulous guardians and conservators often demand that heirs sign something far more restrictive than a receipt, saying, "I've just distributed some money to you, and you acknowledged that you've received it."

Instead, it might contain additional clauses that do everything from making you promise you'll never sue the executor/personal representative/trustee to promising never to say anything that person thinks is negative about the guardian, the conservator, or their respective firms and associates and service providers, in perpetuity.

Those people I know who have signed such agreements seem to regret having done this. They worry that someone connected with the guardian might report them for saying something a bit uncomplimentary about those people or businesses. They're not simply nervous nellies. I know of at least one case where an ex-guardian sued an heir for defamation. The heir was in another state, and it was very inconvenient for the heir to travel. She had to hire an attorney in another state, too.

And while we're thinking about what you can and can't say, even if there's no gag order in your case, consider this: what you write to friends (and what they write to you) might well be subpoenaed. If you write negative things about the guardian or conservator to your three closest friends, a judge friendly to that guardian or conservator might well consider that you have 'published' defamatory statements against that person. Normally, you have freedom of speech. But until things change a lot in the area of commercial guardianship and conservatorship, I wouldn't count on it.

This might really shock you: what you say to your doctor isn't private, either, if the guardian or conservator chooses to subpoena your medical records and a judge allows this. If you are ever involved in a legal contest with a guardian or conservator, you might consider this before you do anything. You might end up being lucky if your doctor has only the electronic records where s/he checks boxes and doesn't write any narrative notes.

You should know this in case you are ever called to give a deposition or be a witness: it is standard practice for the other side's attorney to ask you, after you are sworn in, if you are taking any prescription medication. If you are, this simple fact can be used against you, if for no other reason than to suggest that the drug might have impaired your ability to think straight or otherwise affected your ability to be a reliable witness. And it might lead to further inquiries into why you are taking that specific medication.

There is only one person whose records the guardian and conservator normally can't touch, can't use against you, and can't make public—your attorney. Whatever you write or say to your attorney is considered a 'privileged communication.' Even if the attorney never reads what you sent, as long as you sent it to the attorney, the other side can't commandeer it.

If you want to protect sensitive information, that's one way to do it. You have to trust your attorney not to reveal it to any unauthorized person; it remains 'yours' and can't be used as evidence by anyone except if you express your desire to commit a crime or harm someone. One way to keep private information private is to arrange with your attorney that, if you title an email in a particular way, it's 'for the file only.'

This means they don't have to read it, and you don't have to pay them to read it. After the case is over, they can return all their copies of these emails to you. This is one reason to work only with an attorney you trust completely.

If you reach the point in a case where you make a final settlement, there are likely to be one or more clauses that are favorable to the other side. There have to be. Otherwise, it's not a compromise.

If you're involved in a similar situation, most likely you can get a large chunk of your freedom back, too, if you are careful not to sign your rights away earlier. Or if you signed them away on the basis of false promises, those lies might make the contract invalid.

You have no control over what the judge might decide to do. Although sometimes you can protest and a state supreme court might back you up, your state might decide to take no action to help. Then there's no further recourse for you, other than the strategies I'll cover in the last chapter.

A Ray of Legal Hope

Having the ongoing help of lawyers doesn't seem to fit into the worldview of most families or individuals. They only consult an attorney when potential legal problems threaten to overwhelm them. To me, this sounds a lot like, "I have a pain in my right lower abdomen. It comes and goes, and it's getting pretty bad, but I'll wait until my appendix bursts before I see a doctor."

Just remember: The more trouble you're in before you ask for expert help, the less likely that the outcome will be entirely satisfactory.

It's no mystery why this happens. The average hourly rate for an attorney is about ten times what the average wage-earner is paid for that same hour of work. This places the middle class in a difficult position. Even when they'd benefit greatly from an attorney's advice, they can't afford to get that help on a consistent basis. From the results I've seen most people get, when they try to go it alone, that's not a road I'd ever recommend to anyone.

Although the future looks bleak for those who can't afford an attorney from one of the big law firms, there's good news, too. As I was researching this book, I came across a potential legal answer for the rest of us; by that I mean those who aren't poor enough to qualify for legal aid, but who aren't multimillionaires either. Having ongoing 'legal insurance' might help both elders and those who love them. However, the same firm is only supposed to handle one side of a legal case.

The research I did on this subject has resulted in *Legal Protection: Affordable Options for Individuals, Families, and Small Businesses*. It profiles the best discount legal services of 2023, as evaluated by Forbes Advisor, and I also included a review of a couple of other providers that have been around for a while. The firm Forbes Advisor found best, overall, was LegalShield, a company that now has 4.4 million subscribers. It handles the legal affairs of small businesses as well as individuals and families.[73]

As of this writing, LegalShield attorneys do not serve as guardians or conservators; they are their clients' advocates. If an elder has an ongoing relationship with a LegalShield firm, s/he can call anytime, 24/7, if any legal rights are in jeopardy. Family subscribers can ask questions along the way. They don't have to wait until their loved one is in danger. For any loved ones who are not dependents they need their own subscription.

If you're determined to go to court without a lawyer standing next to you, LegalShield will also coach you on exactly what to say. However, if you don't have an attorney with you, you won't have anyone to help if someone in the courtroom decides to throw you a curveball.

You can find more information in *Legal Protection*.[74]

Conclusion

Just to recap a bit, in this chapter I've explained the individuals relating to the legal process and the general purposes and uses of various documents you might be asked to sign or terms you might be asked to agree to. Be very careful before you sign anything; these papers are designed for the commercial guardian's, conservator's, or trustee's benefit, not yours! I'd strongly recommend never signing anything that a good attorney hasn't analyzed and explained to you first.

You will experience greater emotional pain if you were emotionally close to the ward before the guardianship. If you only saw the ward a few times a year, the guardian will probably do as much as possible to make your rare visits pleasant. For those who were close to the ward, I've devoted the entire next chapter to various ways to help you preserve your emotional health during this difficult time.

TAKEAWAYS

1. Laws and regulations vary from state to state.
2. You are the final judge of what sorts of legal papers you are willing to sign.
3. The best protection is having trustworthy legal and accounting help all along.
4. Expect any opposing legal and guardianship folks to act hostile or try to gaslight you, particularly if you have been emotionally close to the ward or lodged any complaints against them.

CHAPTER VIII
Emotional Support

STRESS THERAPY

With all the negativity that people toss your way, it's so easy to fall into the trap of pessimism!

"Pessimism leads to weakness, optimism to power," said psychologist William James.

But how can people enmeshed in a skewed system maintain even the tiniest shred of optimism? The legal and medical situation in which we and our elders live is constructed to make all family members feel like rats in a maze with no exit. Legal and medical structures reinforce each other. The 'professionals' show a certain amount of respect for each other, but often not for us. What a frustrating situation!

Frustrations abound for both family caregivers and the families of wards with commercial guardians. Both might find the material in the rest of this chapter helpful.

Our frustrations, in turn, make it far easier for those who know how the system works to manipulate family members for the advantage of the professionals involved, and sometimes also for what looks to the others like the benefit of one family member who is most closely collaborating with them. (I suspect that most of those relatives, if you interviewed them five years later, would admit to having been used by the commercial interests, even if they didn't realize it at the time.) Some unethical commercial operators have no hesitation in manipulating entire families.

If you believe in any form of ultimate justice, you have the consolation that people you admire have often been opposed by inimical social forces. There are many examples of grace under fire. William James offers a secular perspective, but his observation tells his readers the same thing. A negative belief structure tends to lead to failure. Obsessing about the inequities of your treatment will tend to blind you to any existing possibilities for escaping your current situation.

Allowing yourself to spend hours and hours bemoaning the current (or past) awful events will only exhaust you emotionally. It will not solve your problems. If you have a job and are too distracted, this state of mind might lead you to make errors in your work. Some people in this situation get themselves fired. Having that happen will harm both you and your loved one, who might be deprived of your company as you search for another job.

It might also depress your immune system and make you sick. If you're ill, you can't help either yourself or your loved one. So, the logical thing is to find other activities to occupy your time. Positive activities.

To quiet that negative voice, you must first calm yourself. The voice I mean is the one telling you that things can only get worse and worse and can never get better. There are time-tested ways to lessen your own feelings of agitation. Whether you do that through prayer, meditation, breathing exercises, making sure you laugh daily, keeping a journal, or some other modality, you can arrive at the same result. You might even make it a point to engage in more than one of those activities.

James is so right! Negativity feeds on itself. If you are going to spend social time, seek out positive, supportive people, not the ones who believe every pending event is a tragedy about to happen. And definitely not the ones you know will blame you for what's happening. You are responsible for how you react to what's happening. You didn't create this situation.

Family Members' Pain—Is It Real?

Do you wonder why I don't often quote what commercial guardians have to say about this situation? That's because I've spent years hearing them tell their listeners that what all the family members of their wards were experiencing and complaining about simply wasn't happening. They claimed we were all imagining it. I continue to hear interviews with commercial guardians, judges, and court administrators during which they say the same thing. "These malcontents are only a tiny percentage of the family members, and the fault lies with them, not the system," they always seem to tell the media.

Would that be true if all the records were open to inspection? Not likely. All of the websites describing abuse by guardians testify either to the pain of an individual or to groups that have sprung up to try to support these family victims of both commercial and state-employed guardians. And it isn't only in the United States that these abuses happen regularly. There have been complaints in Canada[75] and even as far away as Australia.[76]

It's possible for a group of people in one place to think they saw something that wasn't there. Think about the Salem Witch Trials of the seventeenth century, when a group of young New England girls all accused adults in the community of being witches. This was a sort of group hysteria. And that's what the guardians want everyone to believe is happening now. They are all wonderful, saintly beings, they say, and anyone who complains about anything they might have said or done is automatically crazy, or at least hysterical.

Unlike that long-ago experience in Salem, Massachusetts, the complainers now often don't know each other. They come from different states. Their problems occurred during different years. So many similar complaints have been posted! Are they deliberately lying? Are all of those who posted them crazy? Hardly likely.

Family guardians need support too. They need respite. They need understanding. But when a commercial guardian enters the picture, that support for family members needs to be of a different sort. After what I've just revealed, you probably want some emotional support yourself. And if you don't now, and your loved one's problems drag on for years, it's almost inevitable that you will at some future time.

Perhaps the guiding quote for this section should be:

"Adversity is inevitable; stress is optional."

Evangelist Rick Hughes used this statement in most of his sermons. It suggests that, even though the events we experience may be horrible, our reactions can still be positive and even uplifting.

Martial artist Chuck Norris expressed a more secular way of looking at this problem:

"Exercise, prayer, and meditation are examples of calming rituals. They have been shown to induce a happier mood and provide a positive pathway through life's daily frustrations."[77]

If you'd prefer, you can use the more 'modern' perception of Jack Canfield. E+R=O goes his famous dictum. The Event, plus your Reaction to that event, will result in the Outcome. I put the word 'modern' in quotation marks because I find a lot of his suggestions, including this one, seem firmly rooted in the classical Chinese philosophy he studied while an undergraduate at Harvard.

If your loved one has a commercial guardian, confiding in your friends might well subject them to becoming witnesses. Pastors and religious counselors can also be subpoenaed. They might have to appear in court but might or might not be compelled to take the stand.

As if that isn't enough, you have less protection when confiding in an attorney than you used to have. Years ago, an attorney was only supposed to reveal client information to prevent a crime. An attorney's records can now be subpoenaed, and under certain circumstances, he must hand over those records.[78]

Words in legal ethics such as the attorney complying to a "reasonable" degree with subpoenas and other terms used may suggest that the attorney is more an officer of the court than the representative of a client. These now appear in the ABA's ethics statement. If it's difficult to contact the client (or former client), the secrecy requirements are at the discretion of the attorney.[79]

If you're not an attorney yourself, you've most likely never heard this information before. Much of this news likely came as a shock and you need time to recharge your batteries before going back into the battle.

Free Law Clinics

There are places where you can look for support and places where it might potentially cause you harm if you try to search it out. I'll try to help you figure out where to look and what to look for. To cite just one example: in some states there are occasional free law clinics. Theoretically, they're designed to help people who can't afford an attorney with their legal problems. They're for people who don't feel rich enough to hire an attorney. In some cases, even the children of wards who have money aren't all that flush at some points during their lives.

Some years ago, I knew an adult child of one of the wealthier wards; her mother had at least started out with assets in the multiple millions. My friend, who wasn't wealthy, arrived at one of these free law clinics hoping to find an attorney to help her maintain her ability to see her mother, who was then under commercial guardianship. She told the greeter at the door that she needed to see someone about elder guardianship. "I know exactly who you need! He's our go-to guardianship expert at every one of these clinics," gushed the greeter. "You need to see Mr. Smith!" (not his real name) she said as she pointed him out.

Recognizing the attorney at the table about fifty feet away as one of the people sitting on the opposing side in her mother's case, my friend fairly ran out of the room, praying silently that he hadn't seen her.

Unfortunately, other free law clinics might have similar guardianship specialists. They might be attorneys who habitually represent commercial guardians and are perhaps looking for more clients for their clients. They will have what I think of as an automatic conflict of interest. As my friend realized immediately, the commercial guardian would be angry with her for having gone simply to ask for help. Even if that specific attorney didn't report her to the commercial guardian, he would likely use his knowledge that she planned to complain about his clients to my friend's later disadvantage.

(If there is a gag order in your case, you are allowed to speak to a lawyer who isn't involved in the case if you are searching for someone to represent you. The judge can't fine or jail you for consulting an attorney unless there's a court order saying you can't consult that particular person or law firm. Don't laugh. As I've already explained, judges in sequestered guardianship cases do sometimes issue these sorts of orders.)

Stress Reduction Methods

What sorts of stress reduction techniques do other people in your situation use? What might work for you? You will be faced with some hard choices along your journey. Making these choices is likely to stress you out, so you are going to need at least some of these techniques.

Breathing exercises come to mind first. Breathing slowly and gently, and breathing out for longer than you breathe in, has a tendency to relax muscles and moderate your mood. A lot of us remember our mothers telling us, "If you feel angry, take three slow, deep breaths before you say anything!"

It's still true. This is one very simple and often highly effective method of avoiding white-hot rage. Here, however, it will usually be negative thoughts you will need to moderate. Liquor and drugs won't help; when they wear off, the original problem will still be there.[80]

Make sure, in advance, that you are medically able to use these techniques without harming yourself. You will find your own rhythm, but if you're not accustomed to breathing rhythmically, start gently. Don't force anything. Even if all you do is breathe in, slowly, for three counts, and then out, slowly, for three counts, you'll find it slows you down to a state where you can focus. You can then start breathing out for four or more counts.

You will find your own right pace. Perhaps only three repetitions each morning before you try to tackle your day will do it for you. You might even choose to try doing this in bed before you get up in the morning. You can work up to more repetitions over time. If you can space out some deep breathing exercises that continue for two minutes or so three or four times during the day, you will achieve much greater relaxation for your tense muscles. Pick the regimen that works best for you.

Be grateful for the things you love. I can sit and watch the sunrise or sunset over the mountains in a state of meditation and wonder. Doing that renews me. I explain more about why in my course. Sunrise and sunset are just the things I picked to be consciously grateful for. You should pick something that's beautiful to you; something you love. Concentrate on observing all the details you can and being grateful for having that wonderful thing (or person or pet) in your life.

Gratitude is a great way to kill the blues. If you choose to, you can make a habit of doing this every day after your breathing exercises. Being in a calm and grateful frame of mind makes it easier to think through problems and not assume that the worst is going to happen. It rarely does, you know. Often, the very best possible outcome (from your perspective at the beginning, when you first set your goals) doesn't happen, either.

When you accept this, you can get on with the business of living. You can call this going with the flow. Or you can call what happens an answered prayer. It simply wasn't answered in any way that you would have expected. All I can tell you is that it might not feel that way at the time. It might look like "No!"

When it happened to me, I just kept plugging away, doing what I could and praying. What that "no" looks like to me now is, "Have faith! You can do better; you just need to choose a different goal."

Think back on your life. You might be able to find similar situations when you didn't get what you thought you wanted, but maybe you got something different that, in hindsight, is much better for you. There must be millions of people who discover, years later, that if they'd married the person they thought they loved, it wouldn't have worked out at all. There are innumerable ways in which this sort of substitution of goals can happen.

Did what you got ever turn out to be better, in some way, than the goal you had at first? Is there some way it was of more use to you in your journey through life? If you can do this exercise at least once each week for a month, the results are likely to make you far less judgmental of yourself when you can't get things to turn out to exactly match your original goals.

Challenges are inevitable in life. You can't change or grow unless you step outside the orbit of the familiar that some people call your 'comfort zone.' Feeling stress is one possible reaction to challenges. With practice, you can teach yourself to react differently.

Challenge is a more neutral word than 'danger' or 'attack.' Danger suggests that you might need to run; attack suggests (at least to me) that you might have to fight back. If you can redefine each of these events as an opportunity to learn, each challenge will help you grow. Then, you can decide how to react if, in fact, it makes sense to react directly at all.

People whose loved ones have bad guardians often complain of being gaslighted. The personnel involved try to make you feel crazy or stupid. This might be a simple as saying, "The ward's feeling just fine today," when you can see she's flushed and feverish.

They're trying to make you feel stupid and inadequate, and perhaps a bit crazy too. Don't fall for it! They can't use these encounters against you if you don't react in anger or sadness. You may have no control over what a commercial guardian might try to do or say, perhaps deliberately, to provoke you, but you do have control over how you respond.

Get some sunshine and exercise daily. If there's no sunlight, you can use full-spectrum electric bulbs inside your home or office. Check your vitamin and mineral levels to make sure they're optimal. And try to sleep as close to your normal amount of time as possible. This will improve your immune function. Let me repeat this: it is not going to help your loved one if you get sick. Food supplements might replace some of the vitamins and minerals depleted by the pressure you're under. You should consult a qualified practitioner who knows you well to get recommendations.

By now, you can probably guess most of the reasons why a bad guardian might want you to stay away from the ward. There might be some additional ones unique to your situation.

Humor

If your loved one's commercial guardian seems hostile to you, be prepared for a state of ongoing psychological warfare. Humor can protect both your body and your mind. Make sure you take the time to laugh every day.

Decades ago, American journalist Norman Cousins wrote a book called *Anatomy of an Illness*, describing his recovery from an agonizing and supposedly incurable illness through humor. His books are still selling. Why? Because we need them. They were the first of their type, and very good books, too. Medical research took years to catch up with Cousins's perception. It now confirms that humor is the final weapon in your arsenal. Find the time to laugh. That might mean watching a rerun of some silly sit-com or watching a clip of a skit from a favorite comic on YouTube.

Humor helps you maintain a sense of how absurd life can sometimes be. Isn't it ridiculous that people who are all supposed to care about the same person come to such wildly different conclusions about what should be done? You must remain healthy and reasonably well-balanced in your own mental outlook or you won't be able to help your loved one effectively, either. Do not let anyone make you feel guilty for laughing.

You should have various ways of getting physical activity. Use the ones that best fit you. If you have any questions, consult a practitioner.

Don't allow anyone to provoke or cajole you into speaking about your loved one (if the judge has forbidden you to do this). There is no such thing as a secret if more than one person knows it. If the judge has signed a court order that forbids you to give out information on this subject, your friends are not the people who will go to jail or be fined if you violate the court order that binds you; you will.

It's positively amazing how, as soon as a gag order goes into effect, every friend you have suddenly seems eager to know exactly the information you're forbidden to reveal. Take a break from seeing them for a while if you need to. If they keep insisting, their demands should make you question exactly how deep and supportive their friendship really is.

We've now considered things you can do to care for yourself. Some of these involve keeping yourself healthy and others deal with insulating yourself against problems your friends might cause you, even though they might be acting in all innocence. In the next section, we'll look at what respite means and how to use it.

Another caveat: do not share your attorney's strategy. Do not describe these private conversations to friends, relatives, or the media (including on social media and via email). If you do it, you might void your attorney-client privilege. If you do that, you'll have something substantive to be upset about.

Caring for Yourself—Respite

People speak frequently about "respite" or "respite care." Respite is what a primary caregiver needs. It's a break from the responsibility of caring for a dependent loved one. The second term usually describes a situation in which the ward is being taken to be part of some group for a while to a place where there is supervision by a competent professional or someone comes in from the outside to watch the ward for a while in the ward's own home. Often, senior centers or other sorts of communal organizations have a respite care component. In this section, I'll treat both of these situations.

While we're talking about dependency, https://healthandwellness.com reviews medical devices available on Amazon.com. Recently, it rated nine different devices Amazon sells that enable home caregivers to move bedridden charges without injuring themselves. There are devices that help. You simply need to know where to find them, which are best for your situation, and how to use them. But devices can only do part of the work for you.

COVID-19 severely curtailed the availability of respite care. In some areas where the disease was rampant, people from different homes were not supposed to gather. What would you have done if you'd been an exhausted primary caregiver and needed rest but couldn't get it? If you don't rest periodically, you'll eventually burn out.

If you get sick or work so hard that you become too exhausted to function, your loved one will still need the same amount of help and you're going to have to find a replacement anyway. Even if you don't get visibly or physically ill, being overtired and trying to take care of someone with dementia is like trying to drive when you're drowsing off. It might create an unsafe situation for both you and your loved one.

You'll have the same problem getting backup personnel whether you have in-home professional aides or your loved one uses the services of people who work in a nursing home or other facility. If your loved one needs care, then regardless of who is going to do this work, someone must be there to care for them. Getting aides isn't a problem limited to family caregivers, either. Sometimes, commercial guardians aren't able to get home attendants in the category of care they request. Sometimes, the people they thought they'd hired just don't show up.

Does your loved one need the attendant(s) to be present? If it's a life-or-death situation, it might be too dangerous for the person to remain at home. If one or more aides don't show up for a shift at a facility, other personnel can cover for them, at least temporarily. You need to realize, from the beginning, that you will likely not be available 24/7 every day of the year. You might have other obligations. You might have to work. Another member of the family might need your attention. If you tried to give up everything else in your life for the foreseeable future, how long would your own solvency, all your other relationships, and your sanity last? (I'll have more to say in Chapter X about protecting your solvency.)

That said, there are five basic ways—as well as some secondary ways—that you can become a (poorly paid) family caregiver.

When I say this isn't well-compensated work, I mean that the average professional caregiver in New Mexico had an estimated salary of just over $31,000 in 2023, or about $596 per week. This translates to just over $14.90 per hour (for a forty-hour work week). It's not much over the state's 2023 minimum wage ($12 per hour). In New York, the median rate is currently $26.56/hour.

Should you choose this route, you will almost certainly have to provide the state with a detailed plan of care for your loved one. There are now laws governing family members who offer care.[81]

Most times, for the state to get involved, your loved one will already need to be Medicaid-eligible. You would then be responsible to the state as well as to yourself, your loved ones, and your family. Whatever department or service might be involved in paying you will likely place restrictions on you, as well.

Seventy percent of people turning sixty-five between now and 2030 will need long-term care at some point. Insurance company Genworth has a detailed site where you can get information on the normal prices in your state for everything from a month of homemaking services to a month in a private room at a care facility. They also offer a calculator so you can project expenses through 2070. You'll discover, there, that a service that used to cost $4,481/month in 2020 is projected to cost $10,877/month by 2050.[82]

As of July 2021, Ric Edelman reported that the average cost of care at a nursing home had risen to $8,000/month. With inflation, that would have risen to $113,053.96/year in 2024. Generally, the monthly fee depends on the level of service, and in a trend that I saw starting back in 2006, more and more supplies and other necessities are no longer being covered by the basic per-month charge. So, if your loved one needs laundry done, that will likely cost extra.

I want to emphasize, again, that many family caregivers currently suffer financially by having decided to care for a loved one. States that do pay you generally compensate you less than $2,000/month for taking on this challenge. Often in the past, caregivers' attempts to prevent serious financial losses have been unsuccessful. More about this in Chapter X.

Every family caregiver needs a rest sometime. The state might even require you to present to them a plan that proves you've made arrangements for this. Respite care isn't free. Some services charge by the hour, some by the day. You can find typical figures for your state on the Genworth website. Medicare might pay for up to five days at a facility if your loved one is on hospice already. The number of respite days will vary with the program and the plan. Sometimes Medicaid pays if your loved one is already enrolled in it. The National Institutes of Health has a very informative site on this subject: https://www.nia.nih.gov/health/what-respite-care .

The experience of being a family caregiver has changed mightily from what it was years ago: the state reserves the right to vet your health before you start, to see whether it thinks you're capable of doing the caregiving. In addition, if your loved one has dementia, someone who has the authority to make decisions must approve you as a care provider. This suggests to me that the state (or someone named by the state) has the right to hire you, perhaps the right to 'fire' you, and also the right to prevent you from doing the caregiving in the first place.

This seems to mean that someone else will be your loved one's guardian and/or conservator and you will essentially serve at the pleasure of someone in a state bureaucracy or a commercial guardian, regardless of whose money pays for your work.

It appears that the state is doing all it can to take over as people age and become less able to handle their own affairs. Even if you are working for them at a low wage, the state (not your loved one) will decide what happens to that person from then on.

In this section, I've explored what happens when you want to provide care for a loved one, and you need backup. In the next section, I'll be discussing what sort of community you should search for and how to find emotional support during your loved one's journey, whether you do the direct caregiving or not.

Finding Community

As human beings, we need to feel that we're part of a community. How do you find a supportive community? As the German poet and playwright Johann Wolfgang von Goethe wrote, "..to know of someone here and there whom we accord with, who is living on with us, even in silence,—this makes our earthly ball a peopled garden ."[83]

According to DailyCaring, there are currently 14.9 million people in the United States who suffer from some memory issue and 43.5 million family caregivers directly concerned with caring for people over age fifty (as I've said before, some of those with dementia are under the age of sixty-five).

For veterans, the private charity Wounded Warrior Project helps veterans and their family members navigate both the VA benefits system and the military's caregiver benefits program. In addition, it helps to create plans of care for veterans as well as plans to have a successor caregiver in place, should the original caregiver ever become unable to continue.[84]

Some sites aimed at caregivers for civilians have political positions; DailyCaring is primarily concerned with providing information to family caregivers. In my opinion, it offers relatively neutral information. Both of its founders have MBAs and have cared for aging elders themselves. This site provides standard advice on many subjects relating to family caregiving. It has some affiliate links but makes a written promise on its website only to advertise products it believes in.

In an earlier chapter, I told you about the son who was caring for his mother in his home. He was trying to be the dutiful son and never disagree with his mother, but it took a lot out of him. Depending on the stage of dementia, this would be like saying, "Never say 'no' to your nine-year-old!" Although that might avoid any conflict in the near term, sometimes refusing ("NO, Timmy, you can't walk on that railroad tie!")

is the only way to save a loved one from harm. Does it matter if that person is nine or ninety?

The standard thinking is that you must validate, distract, and redirect when you are dealing with what a person with dementia does or says, no matter what they do or say. As someone who has had personal experience attempting to follow this directive, I can assure you that it doesn't always work.

Specific dementia patients, at certain times, are laser-focused on what they want, and no amount of validation and distraction will work. Which means that "redirecting" their attention to something else won't work, either. There simply will be times when you (and your loved one) must deal with the fact that their wishes are going to be frustrated, even if it means that they become temporarily angry or upset.

In my experience, and in that of other people who have loved ones with dementia, social workers are likely to blame you if you are unable to distract your loved one's attention and then redirect it to some other subject when they ask for something they can't have. I go into this problem in some detail in *Protecting Mama*. Although I've heard that the situation is a little more forgiving now, twenty years after my mother's and my ordeal began, I haven't personally seen any evidence that family members are now off the hook if Dad suddenly starts yelling in a restaurant for no reason that you can discover.

How unrealistic the authorities are, expecting that family members will always agree about everything, even when everyone is rational! Not being able to meet this impossible standard when one person in the conversation suffers from dementia creates guilt in the caregiver if there's ever a disagreement about anything or if the elder ever gets upset.

From experience, I can also assure you that sometimes a person with dementia can get upset just sitting quietly in a favorite chair. Some experts still insist that they are picking up on cues from you. Sometimes, that might be true. However, most of the time it's what's happening in their own mind that's upsetting them because nothing at all is happening out here in the physical world. An activity they love one day might become something they hate the next. One friend of mine compared her experience caring for her elderly father to "living with a 200-pound toddler."

If you seek guidance from foundations or traditional sources, you will likely be told that you must have done something wrong. If you try harder, and longer, they say, you will eventually 'get it right.' It's also true that, if you try hard for a long time, your loved one will progress from the aggressive, manic manifestation of dementia to the next stage, which is more passive. The situation might well have been destined to resolve naturally as the disease progressed. It's possible that this change simply showed that the patient had entered a new phase of dementia and didn't come from any technique the "experts" taught you.

The number of caregiver support organizations has burgeoned over the past ten years. Caregiver Action Network lists many different categories of them on its website, ranging from nonprofits that will educate you about "best practices" to organizations offering training for family caregivers. Before contacting one, do your homework first. Who are they? Who do they represent and what is their philosophy? Pick those as closely aligned with your own values as possible.[85] Geriatric care managers, and social workers, and some other professions are required to report unsafe conditions to the state.

Let's say that, after consulting a service or a foundation, you decide that you want to keep your elder in the same place, without making any changes. Remember that the authorities will evaluate you and your family against their own standards. Any re-evaluations will likely cite any areas of non-compliance. Will they be reported to the state? Perhaps.

Remember that these groups are made up of experts to whom the government is likely to listen (and whom they likely support with grant money). You should contact one of the nonprofits only if you agree with their philosophy and truly intend to implement their suggestions.

Before you decide to become a caregiver, please remember to familiarize yourself with the download available from the National Guardianship Association. There are new sets of standards that were published in 2022. There used to be separate publications for family members and commercial caregivers, but now they have been combined into one thirty-five-page publication. It makes a point of the organization's belief that all caregivers should have the same standards, regardless of whether they are related to the person being cared for or not.[86]

They also offer a checklist to see whether you're complying and a bill of rights that they say should be for the vulnerable person. If you're not a member of the organization, why should you pay attention to this group's guidelines? What if you disagree with some of their standards and practices? This is the group that most states with certification will use to determine whether someone is being cared for properly. Their members often help write the state's own guardianship manual.

An earlier edition of the standards I saw emphasized protecting the ward against that ward's grasping, manipulative, and potentially harmful family members. This language has been moderated in the new documents. They're free to download, but you can't copy or sell them without approval and paying a fee to the organization.

Just for comparison, here are the lengths of the requirements for lay guardians/conservators in three different states. California's current *Handbook for Conservators* (guardians are called "conservators" in California) dates from 2016 and runs 318 pages! The most recent edition of the *Revised Guardianship and Conservatorship Handbook* for the State of New Mexico, published in 2022, runs to 182 pages.[87] In New York, the *Guide to Guardianship For [sic.] Lay Guardians* (2011) only runs to 130 pages.[88]

Is it any easier to act as a guardian in New York than in California? Probably not. Guardians must also keep current on law and rule changes.

Most groups will only provide a supportive community for you if you are willing to agree, in advance, to meet whatever conditions the organization wants you to fulfill. They'll support you emotionally in carrying out their instructions, but this doesn't necessarily include finding the money to do what they require.

A doctor okaying a professional's care plan might help you to get paid by Medicaid or a private insurance plan, but then you must continue to follow that plan. If you think you need a new plan, then you'll need to go back to the doctor and get one. The Alzheimer's Foundation also provides online support groups. As of this writing, it doesn't offer an in-home evaluation and might simply refer you to another local organization to get that done.

Religious organizations will often host one or more groups dedicated to congregants whose family members are suffering from dementia. Normally, these are led either by a counseling minister, a priest, a rabbi, or a social worker.

States may have departments with names like "Aging and Disability Resource Center." You can find a nationwide database of them by searching on the internet for programs in your zip code/city or your loved one's zip code/city.[89]

The same guardianship specialists often change jobs. You might find them working for a nonprofit guardianship agency one year, the state the next, and a private, for-profit agency the following year. Having gained experience, they might then open their own for-profit or non-profit agency. The same applies to elder law/guardianship attorneys. Particularly in states with smaller populations, you'll find that most of the specialists in this area know each other, at least by reputation, and they cooperate with each other.

Once you've involved any outside organizations and given them information about you and your loved one, you'll become subject to their standards for how your loved one should be treated. If your arrangements are not to their satisfaction—or if they know that you have not taken their recommendations—they might choose (or might even be mandated by law) to report you.

A man I used to know told me that, back in the early years of this century, he was taking care of his widowed mother. She'd always said that she wanted to stay in the home she'd shared with her husband. My friend looked in on her several times a day, at considerable cost to his professional career. No one else in his large family helped. The social service agency he'd hired to send aides eventually told him, "Your mother's no longer safe here. If you don't put her into one of our care facilities, we're going to report you to the state."

"Just as I realized they were about to report her as being unsafe, she died," he told me. "If she hadn't, I don't know what I'd have done! Mama always told us that she wanted to spend the rest of her life in that home."

Some respite programs have income restrictions; others don't. State Bar Association programs that offer volunteer legal help I've treated in an earlier chapter.

A word about the names of these programs: In New Mexico there's an organization called the Senior Citizens' Law Office (SCLO). Other states may have similar groups. All the other groups to which the state refers, except for the Senior Citizens' Law Office and a free legal service run by the Bar Association, are run by the state. The Bar Association is a private entity and so is the Senior Citizens' Law Office. The SCLO is a nonprofit organization and the Bar Association is a nonprofit professional association. A reminder here: the Bar Association's primary stated purpose is to represent, and advance the interests of, the legal profession.

Think about it: you want to protect your loved one. Most people do want to stay in their own homes, but under the circumstances that applied before they were incapacitated. Or when they say "home," as you saw in an earlier chapter, they might mean a place that is not where they're living now.

Some of them might either still be in denial about their problems that others see or believe that they will somehow get better with time. I knew one woman who, during the earlier years of her dementia, and even after she realized that she had a problem, kept insisting, "I'm getting better. Pretty soon, I'll be well again." But that never happened.

Once any sort of dementia starts to progress, the patients are at some disconnect from reality. Unless we find an instant, magical cure, the situation is never going to go back to what it used to be, so there is no way to meet your loved one's expectations. What's the next best thing, from their point of view?[90]

Facebook has at least eleven independent (private) family caregiver support groups as of this writing. If you join, your posts will only be seen by other people who have signed up for the group, or by the court if their records are subpoenaed. All of their blurbs say that they are non-judgmental, but you might not have any way to know whether the group has biases or exactly who the moderators are.

Last time I checked, the smallest of these groups had 1,000 members. The largest public Facebook group had more than 75,000 members before Facebook shut it down. This should give you some idea how many family caregivers out there who have access to the internet have asked for help. A group's position in this listing is not related to its size. I first became aware of the existence of these groups in 2011. I have no experience using any of them, but you need to know that these resources are out there.

Most nonprofits that started operations a few years ago with grand aspirations of reforming the system have trimmed back their plans. One of the largest folded in 2022. Just as guardianship itself is a minefield, so too is reform.

For those who want all wards released from any restrictions, please notice that, after Britney Spears's conservatorship was dissolved, her problems didn't magically vanish. We now hear reports of a gifted person who still seems to be vulnerable and does not interact with people the way most of the rest of us do. Mental challenges and relationship issues will not disappear if you remove all protection from the individual or if you apply a new label (word) to describe any person who intervenes, trying to protect the person at risk.

We've just considered various ways in which caregivers and family members of wards might look for support from others in their situation. In the section that follows, we'll talk about what happens next.

If your loved one has been having outbursts and you seek guidance from foundations or traditional sources, you might still be told that you must have done something wrong. So, if you can't find community by seeking advice from the usual caregiving organizations and charities, where can you find emotional support? The American Family Caregiver Alliance (AFCA) was a venerable nonprofit operating in California. It used to offer many services nationwide, including an in-home evaluation of an elder's living arrangements, with the aim of keeping people in their own familiar surroundings. Unfortunately, it closed its doors in 2022.

As we've already discussed, under certain circumstances, you might not think keeping your older loved one in the family home is advisable. However, sometimes, it can be downright dangerous.

Social workers, occupational therapists, and geriatric care specialists can provide a safety evaluation for a fee. They are all likely also mandated reporters, so please be mindful of this fact before you call anyone. If the family doesn't carry out the plan made for it by any mandated reporter, if any of them thinks you're responsible for not making the changes, that person might still report your elder(s) to state authorities as being endangered by your lack of action. What happens after that might become very unpleasant for you.

Remember that the authorities will evaluate you and your family against their standards. Agencies, both public and private (including nonprofits), are made up of experts to whom the court system is likely to listen. You should contact one of the experts or organizations for help only if you already wholeheartedly agree with their philosophy of care and truly intend to implement their suggestions.

A doctor's approval of your care plan might help you to get paid to care for your eligible, dependent loved one by a state program, Medicaid, or a private insurance plan. Then, you must continue to follow that plan, but only if your loved one is eligible and/or the insurance company agrees to have a family caregiver. If you think you need a new plan, you must go back through the same process as before to get one. The Alzheimer's Foundation also provides online support groups, but as of this writing, it doesn't offer an in-home evaluation and, if asked, might simply refer you to someone else.

Some respite programs have income restrictions; others don't. The Alzheimer's Foundation awards $6,000 scholarships twice per year to financially challenged families in need of respite care for a loved one.[91]

Here's the problem: the situation is never going to go back to what it used to be, so there is no way to meet your loved one's expectations. All groups dedicated to family caregivers have some care template in mind of the best way to take care of elders. Their bias is toward keeping them in their own homes. Is that what's best for your loved ones and for the rest of the family?[92] In the earlier stages of dementia, it well might be.

As of this writing, there's some confusion within nonprofits attempting to help family members who care about victims of the adult guardianship system. Some want guardianship abolished. Or they want to change its name. Others are seeking alternatives to formal guardianship. Some alternatives already exist, and one is to create an irrevocable trust. However, if anyone complains about the trustee (if complaints are even allowed under the terms of the trust), a court might appoint a total stranger instead of a family member.

In this section, we've considered various ways caregivers and family members of wards might look for support from others in their situation. In the section that follows, we'll talk about what happens next.

Getting Advice from a Survivor

Now we'll consider what happens after your loved one is well along in the process, and you want to have some contact with another person who has been down this path before you.

Sometimes, a 'survivor' of the adult guardianship system is someone whose loved one has already passed on, but sometimes the person you're seeking is only someone who has a bit more experience than you in this area. If you want to consult a social worker or an attorney, you might want to ask whether that person has had direct experience either caring for or being responsible for an elder with dementia. I was fortunate to have had two attorneys with direct experience in this area with elders about whom they cared deeply. I can't emphasize enough what a huge improvement I thought that made in my outcome.

There's an enormous difference between knowing the theory that's in the books and experiencing the events yourself. You might also get some idea how close the specialist was to his/her own elder. If they were in a cold relationship and you are in a warm relationship, their perspective on things is likely not a good match. Some professionals don't want to speak about their personal lives at all. They may consider this the correct stance to adopt with a client. Whether you will be comfortable working with this person in the long run is another matter.

Some nonprofit organizations focus on individual cases or education and legislative reform. They might be able to help with advice or what's called an amicus brief if a case seems to be turning out seriously badly. (An amicus brief is a statement filed by someone—usually someone with legal training who is not directly involved in that legal case—who supports your position.) There are so many problems in guardianship that their resources are chronically stretched thin.

I've already said that secrecy rules in guardianship proceedings. In August 2020, the American Bar Association released a sixteen-page chart showing just how secret various states keep their adult guardianship cases. New York is one of the few where adult guardianship records theoretically need a good reason to be sealed. Nevada is another. Elsewhere, it seems extremely hard to get any information about guardianship proceedings. Miscreants seem to flourish when state laws or state rules forbid the release of information or documents.

In 2010, the National Guardianship Association's website described what it thought was needed to care for a dependent person. Its requirements then ran to a few pages and its ethics statement was short. Today, as I've said before, that's no longer true. As experts, commercial guardians have a clear field in influencing various state requirements for family caregivers and guardians. The more complex requirements are made of family members, the more likely that a family caregiver or guardian will slip up occasionally.

A commercial guardian or conservator likely will err occasionally also, but in my experience, either they seem to pretend they can't possibly ever make a mistake and everyone overlooks the error, or they simply tell the judge the equivalent of, "So sorry, Your Honor! We goofed!"

In one case, this amounted to a $500,000 discrepancy in the ward's accounts from one day to the next, which the guardian 'fixed' by simply changing the numbers in the report. No penalty for the guardian. Not even a letter of reprimand from the judge. What might have happened to a family guardian who'd made an error of this magnitude?

Governments need money now, perhaps more than they did before COVID-19. Social service organizations, like guardianship firms, will need to justify their existence. They will almost certainly be contracted to oversee family guardians for the court. Or their attorneys will. After all, they're the 'professionals.' Their livelihood will drop if they have fewer wards. It shouldn't be too difficult to find imperfections in a family caregiving situation—anything from a disagreement they witnessed between a caregiver and the ward to not following a care plan to the letter.

To their economic conflict-of-interest, we can add all the vacancies in group care situations caused by the deaths of elders during COVID-19. For the first time in years, in December of 2020, I began to hear local elder care establishments advertising for new residents. In 2023, they continued to advertise and added a lot of postcard mailers to their solicitations. One such establishment was forced to close due to the death of all its residents. The facility was sold, and the new owners started up a new care home.

Some guardianship attorneys and commercial guardians might also have a business interest in such institutions. Or they might be part of a partnership that leases property to a person who wants to manage them. I only know of one such situation, for sure. A lawyer admitted to me that she owned and leased three such properties to individuals she knew were operating assisted living facilities on the premises. There are likely more. After all, if this area of the law is their specialty, they might know something about how to do it. They are supposed to divulge such interests to their clients, but how many actually do?

Another lengthy document is the 258-page set of model guardianship and conservatorship laws drawn up by the American Bar Association and distributed in 2017 to state bar associations. They propose giving great latitude to the judge in each case; even more than those jurists have now. The standard of payment for commercial guardians and conservators in that compendium is whatever the judge thinks is fair. Might some judges also invest in care homes or in buildings leased out to assisted living facilities? Might they allow better compensation to their friends?

The ABA's model legislation calls for prior approval for the ward's expenses. Some people think that getting the judge's prior approval protects the ward. However, the judge has judicial immunity. The judge is not now required to know about finances or budgeting. Unless you can prove something illegal was done by the jurist, you can't do anything to discipline a judge for being overly generous with the ward's money unless the guardian states that the money is going to feather his/her own nest. Would any guardian publicly say this to a judge?

In practice, I've never seen a judge deny a commercial guardian or conservator the right to use the ward's funds, the right to sell the ward's property and investments, even the right to dissolve the ward's "irrevocable" trust. This approval protects the commercial guardians and conservators. "We didn't do anything wrong," they can respond when told that $250,000 is too much to budget for the annual non-medical expenses of a single frail elder who doesn't travel. "See, here? The judge approved every expense."

They still have the right to use the defenseless person's money to defend against any charges the ward's loved ones might bring. The problem is that once a judge approves an expense it's next to impossible to challenge it later.

When the ward has no money left, Medicaid will pay. And the commercial guardian will then generally transfer the ward to a smaller guardianship operation, a nonprofit, or a state-operated agency that's paid by the state. Another option is that they will choose to accept whatever payment the state offers for caring for indigent wards. In every scenario, the commercial guardians—and those services that they use—will get paid. Do the institutions and the guardianship firms need a new group to care for? Perhaps.

Given these pressures, it is likely that an increasing number of wards will be removed from the homes of members of their own family or from the care of loved ones who live nearby. If minor technical infractions allow the state to take over, and the records are secret, people are likely to think the worst about the families whose loved ones were taken away. No one would realize that these errors would have been overlooked if committed by a commercial guardian or conservator. This situation tends to perpetuate the stereotype of the negligent or evil family guardian.

An extremely aggressive attorney can make anyone seem guilty. As New York's former Chief Judge Sol Wachtler famously remarked during a 1985 interview, district attorneys could get a grand jury "to indict a ham sandwich."[93] It's amazing the number of attorneys for guardianship firms and even the personnel on their staff who are former district attorneys and assistant district attorneys.

Assessing guilt and blame keeps our legal system and the guardianship infrastructure based on it humming along. They're putting the blame on you and on the other family members of the ward. It's unlikely they'll change their attitude until a new generation of guardians is educated differently and adopts a different mindset. Until then, their attitude is likely to affect both family caregivers and the families of wards.

Even the pro-guardianship-reform groups welcomed more training for family guardians a few years ago. They did this to improve standards and create a consistent approach all over the United States. A few wards might have been helped, but the ultimate result is that a multitude of bureaucratic requirements have now been placed on family guardians. This group is now discovering that they might have unwittingly committed an infraction of page 30, paragraph 3, sub-section "a" of the rules.

It will almost certainly be the National Guardianship Association— an industry promotion organization—that will create the standards family caregivers must satisfy. Or the state branch of its organization will. States might require family caregivers who are guardians to complete the training offered by the Center for Guardianship Certification, but their professional organization is the NGA. They will have written all standards for their own advantage and convenience, not yours. I'm not entirely convinced that they will have written them for the benefit of your loved one.

Here's one example of what I mean. Two wards were at the same stage of dementia. A commercial guardian told the family of one ward that he needed two attendants because he was in his own home and still able to get out of bed. The same commercial guardian told the relative of another ward that she needed two attendants because she was in her own home and no longer able to get out of bed. Are you confused? Does every ward at that stage of dementia need two attendants? These contradictory statements of what's 'necessary,' and the rationales behind them, make no sense when read one right after the other.

Two aides on the same shift would not be the normal home staffing ratio in any home care situation with which I'm familiar. However, it does neatly dispose of a fair-sized chunk of the ward's assets. I know of a deposition during which an expert testified that a medical need for two attendants 24/7 was the definition of someone who required institutionalization and could not safely be kept at home anymore.

This sort of contradictory messaging can only survive behind a curtain of secrecy. That commercial guardian exerted considerable effort to keep different families whose members were under their care from socializing. What credibility did that commercial guardian retain when a member of the first family described above met a member of the second one, and they started talking about their loved ones' commercial guardian?

Many family members of wards barely make it out of the guardianship jungle emotionally whole. Some remain enmeshed emotionally for the rest of their lives. Some simply want to forget their ordeal. Still others have spent years in court battles, exhausting themselves and their resources in the process. Those who've challenged accountings or the commercial guardian's medical choices might have discovered, to their horror, that they've missed some legal deadline or other and can no longer even file a complaint. They will never receive any satisfaction.

Isolated groups of survivors become activists, trying to change the laws for what they perceive to be the better for others coming after them. Based on examining the New Mexico dockets, it looks as if most have been 'gagged' in some way by a multitude of court orders. These are the confidentiality agreements and non-disclosure and non-disparagement agreements I mentioned in the last chapter. They may only be able to tell you certain things but not others. They have never tried to get these orders lifted, so they might be fined or go to jail if they speak out.

If you doubt that our systems are slow to change, consider that the ABA's proposed guardianship reforms, promulgated in 2017, had only passed in two states by mid-2024. I don't believe that always giving the judge more power is wise anyway. It depends on the probity of the judge.

Court secrecy leads to a separate-but-not-really-equal form of court process for those faced with or already in an adult guardianship situation. Some states have created or attempted to create a totally separate court system for seniors. To me, this additional separation and secrecy suggests there's something shameful about these proceedings; something that must remain hidden.

Who benefits? As I said before, the honest people in the industry will gain nothing from secrecy. Those who stand to gain are the predatory guardians and conservators, and other dishonest people associated with the courts in some capacity. Meanwhile, states continue to disagree about what wards need. If those needs were medical necessities, wouldn't there be greater consistency?

What about the family members? If you have a serious illness, an addiction, or simply a need for math tutoring, it's easy to find a peer group. Peer counselors are available for almost any need. Did someone you loved die? Hospice runs support groups.

In the adult guardianship field, however, outside of anonymous Facebook moderators who run secret groups, the enforced secrecy of the commercial guardianship process might cut you off from people who might help you, except if you're in such dire need of help that you approach one of the few nonprofits that interest themselves in posting your story on their website and trying to change the law. But that rarely helps you in the moment.

You can find more web-based attempts to help family caregivers than the families of wards of commercial guardians. That's because there are far more seniors with little or no money than there are with some savings or investment accounts. All Baby Boomers will soon be at the mercy of the commercial guardianship system. Some already are.

In a radio interview on KKOB a few years ago, Diane Dimond discussed her many interviews with the families of celebrities whose elder loved ones had been sucked into the commercial guardianship system. They had all the planners and attorneys they could pay for, but they couldn't escape either.

Now you know why it's so hard to find someone to mentor you, your family, and your loved one through this difficult process. You need someone who won't try to make you feel guilty for events that might be entirely out of your control. It may take years to change the law.

In Chapters IX and X, I've examined how things are done in practice and next we'll see how the media might fit into an already-legal way to improve the situation even before the laws are changed.

Conclusion

It might not be easy to find emotional support. You might approach a nonprofit for help, only to discover that its principles are not in accord with your family's beliefs and practices. Maybe that group believes families are inherently bad. Maybe you find one that considers inheritances terrible things, too. Make sure any organization or counselor you consult has values that support yours. Doing your research first might save you a lifetime of regret.

Remember to care for yourself throughout the process. Pray, meditate, get enough sleep, and stay as calm as possible. You can only help your loved one if you can keep it together yourself.

TAKEAWAYS

1. Explore your most congenial way of exercising, meditating, praying, and finding other ways to relax to figure out what's right for you.
2. Practice gratitude.
3. Research, in advance, the services you'll likely need (explained further in Chapter VIII).
4. Planning for contingencies just might save your disposition (or even your sanity).

CHAPTER IX

When Might You Need an Attorney?

The Myth of the Happy Family and Other Fairytales

"The happy family is a myth for many," wrote British psychotherapist Carolyn Stone.

In this chapter, we'll start by considering the ideal family—the one the authorities seem to want to believe exists. Then, we'll look at various ways many families develop that don't conform to those expectations, and what might happen as a result. (Sometimes, even in seemingly perfect families, a judge voids all the existing documents, anyway.)

As most of us have been told since we were young, "Never say never!" When tensions escalate, if they can't be defused, eventually attorneys seem to enter the picture.

Based on the pronouncements I've heard from judges and attorneys, the government experts seem to expect everyone always to have had an idyllic life with angelic relatives. They have never—or so the story continues—disagreed with other family members. For any differences of opinion, the psychologists, psychiatrists, judges, and social workers think they've found, the family earns demerits.

Court officials and negotiators, and sometimes relatives, often make other family members feel so guilty that they give up inheritances to other relatives or bow to some other family member's idea of what a loved one should do. Sometimes, they call this "keeping peace in the family." How is that peace? Almost certainly, some other disagreements will crop up later. Those same people will demand that the 'losers' last time become the losers this time, too.

Some books counsel relatives to do absolutely anything to avoid going to court. "Give up everything!" they exhort. Those authors are making assumptions about why someone is holding out. Do you want your loved one to live in a way you know displeases them, perhaps even with people they dislike caring for them?

Books on avoiding court-appointed guardianship generally counsel getting the legal papers in order long in advance of any suggestion of dementia. Even before that, you should have learned as much as you can about family finances and the wishes of your loved ones. This means you must have had meaningful conversations with them over time.

If late-life living arrangements, final wishes, and finances weren't part of the family conversation, if they were kept secret, you need to take time as soon as you can and before anyone shows signs of dementia to try to open these topics to discussion . . . but for heaven's sake, not for the first time over Christmas dinner! I was shocked to discover that my immediate family always shared their plans, but my uncle's family didn't. This caused some serious misunderstandings between my cousins and me decades later.

Years ago, I read an advice column in which one writer asked the columnist how to fess up to changing religious affiliations. She answered that part of being an adult is to say, "You know, Mama, I'm not a Presbyterian anymore."

Sometimes, religious doctrine might dictate funeral or burial arrangements. If the reasons for an elder's choices lie in religious convictions, it would help to know this in advance.

Why don't our loved ones tell the whole story? How many reasons are there? I've lost count. Everything from denying our mortality to hiding children from previous relationships has come up in explanations I have heard. With the ready availability of genetic testing, trying to hide relatives has become less and less possible.

The state appears to believe that the ideal family consists of individuals who know all about each other and that the state can ultimately determine the 'right' way to treat a person in need of care without listening to all sides of the issue. The doctrine of "one correct answer" might not be true. Neither might the idea that all family members know the one correct answer. A child born five years earlier might have heard parents espousing different ideas from one born five years later. Both might be telling "the truth" about their parents' wishes as they heard them expressed. A later written values statement might (or might not) be valid, depending on the mental condition of the person who created it.

Unfortunately for the family-model-makers in the court system and their allied experts, many real-world families have members who see each other rarely. One member might not have seen another for several years or longer. One woman carefully kept the changes in her religious convictions from her sister and nieces, fearing an argument. When she developed dementia and needed help, these relatives (who hadn't seen her in years) told the social worker something entirely different from what people who saw her frequently said.

Once an elder is no longer capable of independent decision-making, if everything is not all arranged (and agreed to by all stakeholders) within the family, you have an emergency on your hands. Relatives who tended to disagree with you before probably will do so again.

Now that we've examined the fictional 'perfect family' the state expects to see, we'll walk through how to try to create something that more or less approximates it for the benefit of you, your loved ones, and the state. And then we'll look at what happens when you can't make that out-of-court series of options work for you.

We've examined legal documents in Chapter VII, so I won't revisit that material here.

Before Trouble Strikes (Counseling)

American psychotherapist Virginia Satir said, "Communication is to relationships what breath is to life."

If relatives are not communicating and solving problems respectfully before an emergency, the extra stress created by a sudden urgent need is likely to worsen the situation.

Let me put it this way: if there's an inheritance with three parts and each person is supposed to get an equal share, how does it benefit family harmony for two people to gang up on the third and demand that person give up his share "in the name of family harmony?" To me, that's not harmony. As I've said before, that's bullying. Yet I've heard tales of this happening.

How did it benefit that New Mexico family whose trust owned a ranch for the expected distribution of their inheritances to be changed hours before their patriarch died? Rather than having the lifetime income he'd arranged for all of them, they got a one-time payment only. Furthermore, the person the family patriarch wanted to safeguard their inheritance by managing the family trust was out of a job and out of a home.

Some counselors, social workers, and attorneys offer mediation or family counseling services. If you find one who has no financial interest in or close association with a guardianship-related business, you might have found a sympathetic individual with good professional credentials. LegalShield can often hook you up with an attorney who has no such conflict of interest.

I know of one corporate attorney who left the law entirely based on her perception that it was already too late to save the situation once a case had found its way into court. Her name is Randy Rolfe. She believed that she needed to end her law practice and turn to family counseling instead to try to keep families out of court.[94] I also know of guardianship attorneys who have quit that area of practice on the basis that it was not a level playing field.[95]

If your family disputes can be resolved with a rational discussion that you all have with a counselor, your loved one is probably not all that far down the dementia road. By the time our elders are in an agitated stage of dementia (the infamous Stage 4 of Alzheimer's), it's likely that you won't be able to reason with them and they'll simply get angry if confronted (even in a gentle or oblique way) about what you think are their current problems. Denial kicks in. Buttons are pushed and you're already in trouble.

From what I've observed, rarely is an entire family—by which I mean all grown siblings with families of their own, perhaps a couple of aunts or uncles, parents, nieces, nephews, and perhaps a new significant other in a parent's life—ready to see the same counselor at the same time. And if a parent is denying that there's a problem that everyone else sees, or there are problems that the parent and a new significant other both deny, it's unlikely that the elder will enter counseling willingly.

I've also heard of families where multiple siblings can't agree on how to handle a parent's care. Several of them go to counseling. However, one additional sibling either refuses to go or doesn't keep promises made there. It's likely that this particular sibling has always disregarded promises made to other family members. This just confirms that the way the family solves problems has only worked for three out of four of the siblings. Meanwhile, their loved one's condition has continued to deteriorate. To protect Mama, someone must take more extreme action.

Sometimes, the situation's urgency induces the balky sibling to agree with the rest. And then, hopefully, Mama makes it easy for her children and agrees that their solution is fine with her. Once everyone agrees, they can sign a contract that stipulates they'll all abide by powers of attorney, wills, and/or trust documents. All will be well until one of the siblings changes his/her mind. Perhaps a new problem has arisen, or maybe one of the siblings wasn't all that enthusiastic about the original agreement.

Finally, one of them decides to go to court. Later, they are likely to hear a judge's pronouncements that the whole family needs to be punished for being dysfunctional. I'm speaking here on the basis of repeated statements I've heard from judges and attorneys that only dysfunctional families end up in court, and all the members have to be guilty of something, or they'd never come to court at all. The judge then imposes a commercial guardian on that family; a guardian who shares the judge's negative opinion of the families of wards.

English jurist William Blackstone, writing in 1769, penned a good summary of the underlying philosophy of Anglo-American law. He wrote: "It is better that ten guilty persons escape than that one innocent suffer."[96] Guardianship judges, however, seem to be punishing a whole group of people who are (at least from what I can see) not guilty of any crime for a period that may last for ten years or more. Why, again, does the judge do this? Well, they're all presumed to be worthy of punishment because one member of the family might be suffering from dementia. Having dementia isn't a crime, either.

Blackstone's rule has been used for centuries to protect the inno-cent. Why do judges in guardianship cases feel absolutely justified in doing the opposite of what's considered proper judicial philosophy? In American Courts of Equity (what an ironic name!), not having done anything illegal doesn't seem to protect you anymore. Instead, everything depends on the probity of the judge. To me, this is the opposite of what I learned in school. It looks a lot like a government of men enforcing their prejudices, and not of objective laws that are neutrally enforced.

The secrecy of guardianship proceedings won't harm you if you have an honorable judge; if you have a hostile or prejudiced one, it can mean a disaster—or even a series of disasters—that will haunt you for the rest of your life. I've known of a judge in one case where he'd ordered one of the participants to remain silent, fining him into bankruptcy for speaking with the press. And then the person so punished was unable to complain because his lack of money to hire an attorney prevented it and the gag order itself prevented further discussion with journalists. Because guardianship cases are not considered criminal court cases, the state generally won't provide an attorney for you if you can't afford one yourself. I'll talk more about that later.

You've now seen the way counseling or family therapy might sometimes help in resolving the problem of what to do about a loved one who needs help, and also of what happens if you can't resolve the dispute without going to court. There's another method that sometimes pre-dates the filing of a suit or the holding of a hearing in a court-room—mediation. We'll consider that possibility in the next section.

Mediation

Let's say you feel that you need a more structured, formal process than family therapy or counseling, but you don't want to go to court. That process would be mediation. Mediation attempts to create a permanent solution that everyone involved agrees to. It's not the same as binding arbitration, in which an outside arbitrator's decision has to be accepted, just like a judge's. "An ounce of mediation," wrote expert mediator Joseph Grynbaum, "is worth a pound of arbitration and a ton of litigation."[97]

A word about the money: commercial guardians use money from the ward's estate to pay their legal bills in almost every instance. Sometimes, they hold money out of the estate, with court approval, specifically for this purpose. The other side will pay their own attorney fees and half the mediator's fee. Then, the ward's estate pays for the other half of the mediator's fee and all the guardian's legal expenses. So, all that money ends up coming out of the heirs' pockets. Some people think this situation isn't fair.

In mediation, the mediator's supposedly disinterested suggestions for a solution can ultimately be accepted or rejected. If they're rejected, you end up in a courtroom, with a judge presiding.

I've had two good experiences with formal mediation, but neither of them was part of the early stages of a guardianship case. In New Mexico, there's supposed to be at least one attempt to hold a mediation before a case goes to trial. Other states may have other rules.

Maybe it's just me. Those mediations involved property, not people. Except that in the second instance, my primary aim was to not lose the freedom of speech that the judge had just returned to me. I'm not sure it would have been as simple for me to spend a few hours resolving a highly emotional issue like the guardianship and living arrangements of a loved one.

Each step in a structured negotiation has a specific task to accomplish. Professor Randy Lowry of Pepperdine University developed a five-step process used by many mediators. Here's the sequence, as I experienced it:

1. One of the attorneys contacts a mediator. Both sides have to approve that mediator. Both sides send a short outline of their arguments to the mediator. They may have short phone discussions with the mediator, and they set a date to meet. Here, the mediator is testing the willingness of the parties to try to come to an agreement. Mediation is not free; the attorneys also have to agree on a budget.

2. Opening Session. The opposing parties are in separate rooms. The mediator lets each individual/group know what

to expect. He (both of my mediators were male) asks each side for a candid assessment of what it wants to achieve. (I'd suggest, here, that if people you're dealing with have been less than candid before, they might not be again and you'll all be out even more money than before, since many mediators are either attorneys or retired judges. It's a chance you take.)

3. Communication. Some mediators do bring the opposing parties to the same table briefly to present their arguments. Some don't. In both mediations I participated in, I was never asked to spend time in the same room with the other side, although in the second case I did see the whole retinue on the other side arrive, both before mediations started and again after lunch. There were multiple law firms involved, as well as the defendant.

4. Negotiation. There may be repeated offers and counteroffers. My first mediation lasted about an hour. The second one lasted from 9:00 a.m. to 4:00 p.m., with some time off for lunch. If you go this route, remember that you are paying your attorney (or in this second case, I was paying two) as well as the mediator for these hours. And the other side is paying its attorneys, too.

5. Finalizing the agreement. This is another task. The mediator will present a draft, or one of the attorneys involved will. You need your attorney to look it over to ensure that what you're signing means what you think it does.

If they've come to an agreement, both sides sign a statement that goes to the judge and says they've agreed on terms. If the judge has no objection, the case is over. The judge almost never objects.

Most of the time, the precise terms and even a discussion of what happened in the mediation rooms during each settlement discussion remain confidential, even if all the documents that were submitted during the discovery part of the case are available to the public. Some sort of confidentiality is usually part of the settlement itself and is considered a separate and enforceable contractual agreement. You can be sued if you talk about the details of a settlement after you promised not to.

If you plan to engage a mediator, research particular negotiators, and research them well. (But remember that both sides must approve of the same mediator.) If you have a good attorney, s/he probably knows who's available in your area, and can tell you something about that person's reputation.

Mediators are frequently attorneys, although most states don't require mediators to have a law degree.

Any attorney who speaks ill of a fellow attorney might be censured by the Bar Association because it's an ethics violation, but that doesn't mean you can't search for signs. A little hesitation in the voice or an involuntary shrinking back in body language during the discussion might give you a clue. You need to be aware of this because sometimes, former judges are *former* judges for a reason. They might have done something that resulted in them having to resign from the bench to avoid being kicked off of it.

Over the last decade, more people have been trying mediation voluntarily. It involves lawyers and judges, but it isn't as formal as a courtroom situation. It doesn't take many years to reach a conclusion, the way most court cases do these days. But the mediator doesn't see as many documents as a judge is supposed to read, either. Both sides send him only the ones they most want him to see. Part of the mediation fee pays for their time spent reading the documents.

The Academy of Professional Family Mediators was founded in 2011-12, as a more specialized spin-off from other mediation organizations. The founders intended to create an organization to set standards in this field. When I checked that site recently, it hadn't been updated after 2017. I have no experience with any of their mediators. There are, of course, many other places to find mediators. However, when I searched among groups I knew, I often came up with attorneys I'd heard complaints against that were related to estates and guardianship issues.

As with judges, if you get a good mediator, be extremely grateful. There are no written records of a mediation outside of the final agreement. No transcripts. The details of each mediation are usually kept as secret as most guardianship cases, so if you happen to get a bad mediator, I'm not sure how you'd complain.

One major problem with mediation is that, as with family therapy, if you are attempting to use this avenue prior to anyone filing a court action, everyone must agree that there's a problem before you even try to engage a mediator. That mediator almost certainly has no power to declare someone mentally incompetent. (State law usually requires a medical person to certify this diagnosis first.) There are far fewer restrictions and requirements for accepting evidence in mediation, and no evidence is kept. So, if you want to go back over—or even complain about—the process later, you can't.

Mediation should work best in cases where a cooler head (a mediator, for instance) would quickly realize that the elder is perfectly well able to manage alone, but some malignant person is trying to take away this elder's freedom for personal gain. In that situation, it might become a valuable tool for saving that elder from a life of confinement and restriction.

However, in the numerous cases I know of where elders have harmed themselves already due to their dementia and can't safely be left alone, they may still be insisting that they are perfectly capable of driving or staying alone when doing so clearly places them (and sometimes others as well) in potential danger. They simply might not remember their brushes with danger.

Or perhaps they'll forget that they can no longer understand money, but they still argue that there's no reason to change anything about their accounts because they're perfectly capable of managing their finances. Their insistence that nothing is wrong, in these situations, I believe, results from their dementia.

The time for someone to sign a power of attorney is when that person is fully competent. Anything signed after a person cannot make a rational decision might be legally invalid or easily voided in court. From all accounts, that was what happened to talk show host Wendy Williams. Only after her son already believed she needed help did he approach a bank official and say his mother couldn't function and he should be appointed to have power of attorney. But the court can't appoint anyone to have power of attorney. It can only appoint a guardian or conservator, and that was exactly what happened.

A human being who cannot make rational decisions will remain in personal and financial danger until the situation improves (if it ever does), but that person might well continue to insist that nothing needs changing. Everything, they say, is just fine. But it isn't. The better you know that person, the more you care about that person, the more upsetting this situation becomes.

At some point, your loved one might end up immobilized in the emergency room after an entirely preventable mishap, with a doctor or nurse asking adult protective services for an investigation into whether they've been neglected or abused, because they're clearly in need of assistance. Judging from the way the elder is interacting with medical personnel, they can clearly see that that person's disconnection from reality must have been present for some time before the accident.

So, now we've completed a tour of what's available to you outside of taking direct legal action through the courts themselves. In the next section, we'll discuss the legal route and what it entails.

The Legal Route

Let's assume that you're now fighting your way through the maze that is our US legal system. Maybe your loved one has a commercial guardian, or the state is hassling you about a family guardianship situation, or your loved one has no money and has somehow been placed into a state-run guardianship situation. Another possibility is that your loved one has already passed away, but the state considers all records relating to the guardianship secret. There may be various 'legalese' words used for this. Two of these are "gagged" and "sequestered."

After all, the defenseless person is or was your relative. You'd like to have some answers about what is happening or might already have happened. Here, I can't speak as an attorney; I can only use my own experience and the experiences of people I know who were able to speak to me at the time they told me what was happening in their lives. Everyone I knew who continued to retain an attorney from within the guardianship group after their loved one died has told me they regretted doing so.

In *Protecting Mama*, and in the Dayspring Empowerment Course, I explain why and how I began the transition from an attorney within the guardianship community to someone outside, years before my mother passed away. That was how I avoided any problems that came from what I regard as the excessive collegiality I witnessed in New Mexico. And I managed to do this with the cooperation of the attorney whose practice I was leaving.

I had to find someone creative, not a club member, and who wasn't afraid to go up against the club. A good litigator costs money. If a good LegalShield-affiliated or recommended litigator takes the case, the process will cost you 25 percent less money.

You can't afford to be dependent on a single source of income during a court case. What if you lose your job? More about how important that is in Chapter X.

If you choose to go to court but you can't get a foundation or someone working on contingency to fund you, then you will want to plan ahead financially. The costs of an expert conducting litigation on your behalf in our legal system seem designed for the budgets of corporations with deep pockets, not for individuals. This is one reason why family members of normal means, and even the relatively affluent, are at a huge disadvantage when in court fighting a corporate guardian, a conservator, or a trustee. You'll need access to money at least in the tens of thousands, if not the hundreds of thousands of dollars. Sometimes even more.

Here's what you're facing: a very well-entrenched system, with norms that seem abnormal to most neutral observers. Journalists, among others, have been astounded by the secrecy surrounding these proceedings. If family members are often excluded from guardianship hearings, how much rarer is it for a journalist to be allowed to attend? One journalist I know was given prior special permission to attend a guardianship hearing recently, only to be told, during the proceedings, that she was expressly forbidden to report in her newspaper any of the statements made during the hearing itself!

That situation makes no sense to me, although I'm told the judge was far more civil to the family member of the ward at that hearing than he ever had been before, and more so than at later hearings, when the journalist wasn't present. Even making things a tiny bit more transparent might be a great help to the families of wards, and also to the wards themselves.

Famous litigator Melvin Belli said, "A lawyer's performance in the courtroom is responsible for 25 percent of the outcome; the remaining 75 percent depends on the facts."[98]

I've hired more than a dozen lawyers (for different reasons) during my life—eight of them during Mama's guardianship and its aftermath. From what I saw during my fourteen years of observing our legal system extremely closely, while trying to protect my mother and follow her wishes, I think that Belli might be emphasizing the wrong part of the process. I've come to believe that most of an attorney's effectiveness comes from what he's able to accomplish outside the courtroom itself.

Why am I saying this? According to Duke University, 98 percent of all civil litigation cases are concluded without a trial! This means your attorney is almost certain to resolve your complaint by hammering out an agreement of some sort with the other side. Perhaps Belli's percentages are correct for the small percentage of the cases that do end up at trial. So, you need an expert negotiator who isn't afraid to fight like a banshee at trial on those rare occasions when this is required. Or maybe your litigator is a knight in shining armor, depending on your perspective.

Not every attorney will accept every case. It's hard to go up against colleagues who all have one point of view while you hold another. I had one attorney who refused to litigate against her colleagues, although she was willing to negotiate. One family member of another ward also told me his attorney had warned him that he'd help, but only to a certain extent, because he had to continue to make a living in that town after this client's case was over.[99]

No one can guarantee the outcome of any honest legal process. It depends—on the judge, the jury, the expertise of your attorney, the expertise of the attorney(s) on the other side, and perhaps on the mood everyone is in when negotiations are conducted. I'm not sure the weather is also a factor, but it might be.

I'm guessing that the advent of artificial intelligence (AI) is likely to change things a bit. Thompson Reuters owns Westlaw, a 150-year-old research database widely used by attorneys. It recently created a waiting list of law firms to get demonstrations of its AI contract analysis function. Recent studies have shown that AI is better at analyzing contracts (and other agreements) than human attorneys are. Its percentage is up around 10 percent better than humans, now, and will only improve as it learns more.[100]

At top law firms, an attorney's employability often depends on the number of hours billed. The more hours s/he bills, the more valuable s/he is to the firm. If a non-disclosure agreement that used to take two hours to review now takes fifteen seconds, how will that attorney justify their continued employment? The smallest billing increment for attorneys is currently six minutes. AI could likely write an entire book in that block of time.

Would you really want to pay $1,000 to a law firm to get a secrecy agreement analyzed when you knew a computer could spit out a detailed analysis in seconds? If your personal attorney spent five minutes going over the AI's analysis, it would probably be 'a lot of time.' In this era of financial uncertainty, corporate and other affluent clients will probably start screaming first.

I'm sure the subscriptions to these AI legal services will be expensive. All subscriptions lawyers have to legal services are expensive when viewed from a layperson's perspective. Will law firms start billing by the second? Is there any way for them to analyze so many documents using AI that they can maintain their previous income? Maybe law firms will develop 'packages' so that it costs $500 for a will, $1,000 for a trust, and $5,000 to analyze a settlement agreement. Then, you will pay them a set fee that does not break down their time.

The only way they can still make astronomical sums will be in court, and during the preparation for a trial, when they can continue to bill on an hourly basis. (Some law firms offered per-project packages before AI, but generally not the big prestigious ones.)

This rapidly approaching new reality suggests to me that, if all these 'extra attorneys' aren't fired out-of-hand, there will be more of an emphasis on forcing cases before a judge to justify having all of the newer associates sitting in their law offices bucking for partner. It will take next to no time to 'write' offers and 'analyze' those offers, because AI will be doing it. If you're an attorney, settling might no longer be in your best interests. Your firm might go broke if you settle enough cases. More active cases that don't settle mean more of a delay in getting them heard by a judge. It can already take years until a case is decided, and I suspect this situation will only get worse.

Regardless of who does what to whom, if there's a gag order in your case, and you violate it, expect to be punished. Whatever satisfaction you might find in seeing your document (or yourself) quoted in the press will be fleeting. There might be a few people in this country who can get away with doing this, but the odds are most emphatically not in your favor. I suspect that perhaps less than one percent of litigants might be able to get away with this tactic, if that many.

Gag orders and any other attempts to keep information from the public are your mortal enemies. Let me share with you the difference between a secret trial and a public trial (*in the same case*):

The case of Mama's estate, with me as its executrix (in New Mexico, we're called "personal representatives"), brought against her former guardian had lasted for five years. I was under a strict gag order for three of those years and an informal gag order the rest of the time.

After the judge lifted the gag order, that case settled within the next two months! That was all the time it took to engage a mediator and schedule a session.

Most probate cases are public by default. That's one of the reasons many people want to avoid probate; they want to avoid sharing any financial information with the public. But it's been my experience that the light of day is the best disinfectant and frees everyone to speak the truth.

Under some circumstances, families might have no recourse for improper things they believe a commercial (or any state-appointed) guardian might have done. Here's an example from Canada:

In 2017, the Province of Nova Scotia adopted a new law.[101] It abolished the word "guardianship." Anyone that US law would have considered "incapacitated" (they are called "adults with intellectual disabilities" in Canada) would henceforth come under the control of a public guardian appointed by the state. No recourse or objection was allowed because, in the state's opinion, it was far better able to make decisions for that elder than any mere family member. Families officially no longer had any special say over the treatment of their loved ones in Nova Scotia. From then on, they would not have any input into decisions regarding either living arrangements or money.

One special peculiarity of the Nova Scotia law, in my opinion, is this statement on the official website: "Making risky or unwise decisions does not mean that an adult is unable to decide for themselves."[102]

Some people want the word "guardianship" deleted from the laws in the United Sates also. They consider it pejorative. Be careful what you wish for—you might get it. In the same sense that the fairytale princess finds her Prince Charming, and then discovers that, after marriage, she will move into the palace not only with her new husband, but also with her mother-in-law, who will still be telling Prince Charming what to do, just as she did before their marriage.

The Media

Some people think that going to the media will solve their problems. *If only I can get a blogger or a journalist interested, I'll be home free!* they tell themselves. If you go that route, do so carefully and not hastily. Have your facts in order. Remember that you also need to make sure you have the right to show the documents to someone outside of your loved one's case.

I was one of those extremely fortunate relatives of a person under guardianship. I had journalists on my side. However, I never approached them. Instead, they approached me. And even then, I had to wait until the judge lifted my gag order before I had any conversations with them. Why? As I've said before, I had no desire to spend time in jail or to go bankrupt. My gag order promised either or both punishments, at the judge's discretion, for any violations of the gag order that I committed.

Journalists can make abuses known, but it's up to the executive branch of government, the courts, the public, the legal profession, the legislature, and our educational institutions to take care of the details of changing attitudes and enforcement.

Once more, I was also lucky that I had an experienced attorney to interpret the court orders for me. In my opinion, you must have someone available who knows how to read legal papers and interpret them so you know exactly what's required of you and don't get yourself into trouble without realizing it. Then, if you become a martyr, you will have chosen that course of action deliberately.

In the final chapter, I'll discuss potential ways to remedy some of the worst aspects of the current situation.

Conclusion

Going to court should always be the last alternative after you exhaust all other remedies. In our current legal system, knowing when and how to ask the courts to intervene is an art, not a science. The other side will have its experts. If you have experts in your corner all along the way, you and your loved ones are better protected.

Do not confuse counseling with mediation or mediation with arbitration or binding arbitration. Unless you have agreed, in advance, to binding arbitration, no order is final until a judge signs it, providing that no one appeals that decision. Then, you can likely measure "final" in years and tens of thousands of dollars. Understanding both the good points and the limitations of each method of solving disputes will give you greater security as you reach that part of the process.

TAKEAWAYS

1. Continue to do your research.
2. Be sure that you understand what counseling, mediation, and arbitration are supposed to accomplish.
3. Get as complete an understanding as possible of what the form of action you choose requires in terms of time, energy, and money before proceeding.
4. Understand that the press can expose problems, but it will almost certainly not be able to solve them.

CHAPTER X

Where Do We Go from Here?

In this final chapter, we'll examine various ways to improve guardianship. Working with the media, educating the industry and the public, and finding ways of telling a personal story so others will listen (and you won't get into trouble) will all help. There are a few other alternatives, too. There's a lot of information in this chapter from Florida. That's simply because Florida has so many residents over sixty-five.

The Court of Public Opinion (Including Education)

Changing the legal system's seemingly longstanding prejudice against families is a long-term goal. The same for social workers. I once saw one lauded in her obituary because she routinely tailed families watching for anything 'wrong' that she could report. There are unkind words for what she was doing. It might even have been illegal.

News flash to The System: relatives don't all and always function as if they were separate countries engaged in permanent warfare with each other. A few might. Most don't. In my opinion, most forms of dysfunction are not illegal (and should not be punished by the courts), and many are remediable.

The idea that humans are imperfect beings is not new, but somehow, we've lost sight of reality in the legal system's quest to achieve impossible standards. Most of us are aware of our imperfections. I suspect that those of us who are aware are almost always trying to improve.

Changing some of the established curricula in law schools and social work departments is a fervent wish of mine. Perhaps social science curricula, as well. Victims of the current system should be introduced into the mix to educate budding attorneys and social workers about how they sometimes come across to the public and to improve communication among attorneys, social workers, and clients.

Some people are great storytellers. They don't let their emotional connection to the events get in the way. If you're one of those people, and you've been through this experience yourself, you should be letting others know about our failed elder care and guardianship system on panels, in podcasts, in law schools, in social work departments, and maybe also at medical schools and bar association meetings.

I firmly believe that if those 'professionals' had to deal directly with us, as fellow humans just telling verifiable truth from our perspective, we might convince them to modify their stance. However, to present documented stories, we'd need to make public the evidence from guardianship proceedings, most of which is now kept strictly secret by the courts.

Seeing family members only in court or when we are being accused of some real or imagined infraction allows 'the other side' to portray us to others as less than human. It's easier to discriminate against someone you never have to face in a social or quasi-social setting. We must band together to make abusive guardianship of wards and mistreatment of their family members an outmoded concept. We need to be visible.

We must find a way to make ourselves real to these industry workers, particularly to the newer generation of social workers, doctors, and attorneys. They're likely the ones we'll deal with when our time comes to be in their sights. We should continue to remind them that they will one day be where we are now, and where our elder loved ones were before us.

We can work together toward a solution. Having only one or two members of reform commissions who have or had family members under guardianship is now the rule. I still think that family members should constitute the majority on any state- or nation-wide guardianship reform committees or commissions. More family members will have their lives affected by the proposed reforms than any other 'stakeholder' group on that panel.

If we are basing our reform on the notion that the majority rules, there are far more of us than of them as I've said before. As we speak, we can also remind them that most of them also had parents, grandparents, and other older relatives and friends. Were they fighting each other and jockeying for position all the time? If not, then why assume that this is necessarily the case in everyone's family except their own?

How can the appearance of cronyism that the judges, attorneys, and social workers now have in guardianship cases be moderated?

One way would be by assigning every person—guardian ad litem, court visitor, and medical professional—randomly to cases. Judges are already supposed to be randomly assigned to cases most of the time.

Even if they're chosen by lot, if the same pool of willing participants continues to serve, over time they might become a cohesive group again.

The biggest factor in reforming the system in the present would be to hold all hearings in public, by default, rather than behind locked doors, except in cases where to do so would endanger the prospective ward's health. By this I mean someone in a hospital room after a serious accident, someone suffering from lifelong mental challenges, or a person who is severely ill, perhaps even with a communicable disease.

Protect Yourself While Working for Change

There's one simple way to protect yourself and everyone you love against being placed under guardianship with no warning: have contact information for your named powers of attorney always accessible. A little card in the front of your wallet will go a long way toward seeing that you are not placed under guardianship, should you ever be in an accident or fall unconscious. Make it easy for hospital personnel to find, not behind the locked screen of a cell phone.

If you don't, then when you wake up, you might already be under the control of a state-appointed guardian in an institution that isn't the one you were taken to in the first place. Once you lose your freedom, you might have a very hard time getting it back. You see, hospitals must free up bed space as fast as possible. If you are in a hospital and can't respond to questions, they can get the court to create an emergency guardianship and appoint a guardian while you are unconscious or unresponsive.

This is exactly what happened to Douglas Hulse, an eighty-year-old retired Florida pilot. In 2020, while pulling into a gas station, he suffered a stroke. The station called 911. Hulse apparently was unable to tell the hospital about his relatives, who all lived out of state. Nothing in his medical file designated a power of attorney. The hospital said they saw no evidence that he had family. Hulse lived alone.

Hospitals aren't allowed to discharge patients into unsafe surroundings, and Hulse would no longer be safe living alone.

The hospital had a commercial guardian appointed. She moved Hulse to a nursing home and started selling off all his belongings, including a collection of memorabilia from around the world that he'd amassed during his aviation career. After he lost contact with his remaining family, they started searching for him. Realizing, through legal research, that her uncle was involved in a guardianship proceeding, his niece managed to contact a guardianship reform advocate.

Then, she finally discovered where her uncle was. She and her brother were once again able to see him on FaceTime.

Hulse, however, was still under guardianship. Ultimately, complaints were filed against the appointed guardian for the improper handling of her power over Hulse, but no action was ever taken. Hulse died soon after, still under guardianship.[103]

Knowing that this is a potential hazard, some law firms that hold signed wills and completed power of attorney forms now give clients pre-printed cards stating, "In case of emergency, please contact XYZ law firm." The client then carries the card whenever leaving home. If nothing else, it puts the hospital on notice that the person has a lawyer, which might make them more cautious about instituting emergency guardianship proceedings before making all possible efforts to contact interested parties.

If you hold someone's power of attorney and are using it, keep detailed records. Get professional advice on what you're allowed to do. If you're not a CPA, either hire one or use a dedicated, specialized computer program to keep track of the money and the medical records, if applicable. Nothing is more likely to cause litigation than other interested parties who believe you have been withholding information from them. Excluding interested parties during POAs, trusteeships, guardianships, and conservatorships can fracture families. Protect yourself.

Years ago, people posted photos of their dinner plates on Facebook. Privacy was not their goal. It was as if they wanted everyone else to know each thing they did, said, and thought all day. Now, it's texting, Instagram, X (formerly Twitter), or another platform that sometimes accomplishes those same goals. However, if you write negative statements about a guardian and send them in an email to three or four friends, that might also be considered "publishing" an opinion. According to the *Cambridge English Dictionary*, this is still "publishing," whether you get paid for that information or not.[104]

Your emails can (and I promise you will) be used against you in court if you say very negative things you can't prove about a guardian or conservator. If you ever get into a court case against a guardian or conservator, they'll likely try to subpoena anything you might have written, and then introduce your statements about them into the record. They might also make a claim against you that you've defamed or libeled them.

The same thing is true of whatever you write in a blog, a tweet, or a comment on someone else's blog, or if there are quotes attributed to you in an article someone else wrote. If you are writing an online review of a guardianship, home care agency, or a facility, don't count on a false name to protect you, either. It won't.

Isn't refraining from saying negative things about someone else a form of self-censorship? Yes. I'd suggest asking for an attorney's opinion if you plan to post a seriously critical review to have some assurance that you aren't inviting your target to sue you.

Real people often suffer for voicing their opinions. Here's what happened in Florida:

The daughter of a man under guardianship kept complaining to anyone who would speak to her about it, as well as on social media. She told everyone that her father's court-appointed guardian was mistreating him. Her many complaints to state agencies resulted in no charges being filed. First, the guardian banned her from seeing her father, then the court slapped her with a gag order. Things escalated and the court ordered her to have no further contact with either her father's guardian or with the guardian's attorney.

Finally, the guardian sued the daughter for slander. The judgment, rendered in August 2018, required the daughter to pay $160,000 to the guardian. Most of her net worth was tied up in her home, so she didn't have enough cash. The court ordered the sale of her home to pay the judgment. After tens of thousands of dollars spent on legal fees and multiple pro se petitions, the daughter managed to retain her home.

Not long after that, her father's guardian was arrested and charged with multiple felonies, including thefts from other clients. That fact did nothing to improve the original whistleblower's position or to compensate her for her pain, suffering, and financial losses.[105]

Theoretically, if you live in the United States, you have the right to express your own opinion. (Other countries have other laws, so if you live elsewhere, be sure to check on any possible local restrictions.) I was very careful while my mother was alive and she had a commercial guardian. The guardian had made it just about impossible for me to see Mama for almost three years and I didn't want that experience repeated. I was always afraid they would banish me again because, every day, I could sense the hostility of the people they hired when I visited Mama.

During discovery in the estate's case against Mama's former guardian, I was somehow not shocked to discover a letter in the guardian's email files proving that her guardian was searching for ways to prevent me from seeing Mama again. The firm's attitude that I'd felt in my gut for years turned out to have been true.

Families are messy and complex to deal with, as almost anyone who grew up in one can attest. Looking at the situation from the commercial guardians' point of view, it makes their job a lot easier if family members don't involve themselves in their loved one's care. I also wonder whether—in addition to wanting to protect their revenue stream—they don't also become a bit possessive of their ward, even without realizing it.

If you don't plan to be involved in a court case with the guardian and/or conservator, and you make negative statements, but you can't prove any of them, they can still sue you. And they can use your loved one's money to pay their legal fees. This happened a few years ago to someone in Arizona. (In Arizona, you only need to communicate a negative untruth to one other person.) The truth is supposed to be a defense. But if the only proof of what you're saying is inside of a sequestered case, and the court won't allow you to use those documents, you have no way to defend yourself.

If you need to use documents in a sequestered or gagged case to prove that you are not guilty of libel or slander, or to prove anything else, the safest thing to do is to make sure those documents are legally available to show to people first. If they're still sequestered, a judge might well refuse to allow you to use them in your defense in a libel or slander case in open court. A judge might even prevent you from using them in a separate *sequestered* case relating to any matter whatsoever.

I've seen websites started by people bent on attacking the entire guardianship industry. Some of the claims I saw there I knew to be false, but I couldn't write or post any corrections because I was living under a gag order at the time. I was convinced those words were written out of pique and pain, sometimes even based on false assumptions.

The posted essays were published under pen names. I haven't heard whether the authors were ever sued for what they said. If they ever received a warning letter from an attorney, I never knew about it either. The website essays were posted in 2016-17 and have since been taken down. I've yet to hear that these negative essays either materially helped any author's own situation or improved anyone else's legal position.

You need to know, before you consider contacting the media or posting anything anywhere, explaining how awful your loved one's power of attorney or guardian or conservator or trustee might be, exactly why you are doing this. Is it to get a problem noticed (and possibly solved)? Have you concluded that specific laws create abuses and so need changing? If you think so, are you certain that the law itself, and not a judicial rule or a court custom that routinely misapplies that law, is the cause of your woes? I wonder whether most of us are even familiar with all these aspects of legal practice that are not part of the statutes themselves.

Do you want sympathy? Are you after revenge? A final possibility to consider is that by knowing what happened in your case, others might be able to avoid the traps you encountered. You get some extra brownie points for your altruism if you check this box.

Is there a real likelihood of you being involved in a lawsuit with the people you are criticizing? There's a national law firm that specializes in working with men who are in the process of getting a divorce. It warns them, in its broadcast commercials, not to post anything the other side can use against them. Same here.

Let's say that your loved one's guardianship case is over. They've passed away and you feel that you need to vent. The gag order has not been lifted. All those years of misery have you fuming. Do you have a fair amount of money? Even if there's little or no money involved, do you have a sense that the other side wants to make an example of you? If you speak out, it's still possible that you can be sued for violating the gag order.

In my experience, some courts seem to want to let everyone know how powerful they are by fining and citing otherwise helpless members of the public. Are you willing to take that chance?

On the other hand, I do know of one family member of a ward who had already been forced to declare bankruptcy as one of the consequences of a long-running, sequestered legal fight with her mother's guardian and conservator. She cooperated with the media, showed them the documents from her mother's case, and got a lot of good press coverage of guardianship abuse issues as a result. Even so, most later reform attempts aimed at correcting the abuses that articles about her case had exposed were ultimately derailed by guardianship industry interests.

Where Things Seem Headed

In my opinion, if things continue going in the same direction, and the courts keep family members in the same inferior position they're in now, we are headed into a period of increasing state control and court-imposed decreasing family involvement. Remember that guardianship interests operate on a global scale. They'll normally start changing laws and rules in that direction in a 'smaller market' (like Nova Scotia) first, and then try to use them in a larger market. I suspect that some of the recent changes in Canadian law provide a clue to what we can expect here.

So, what happens if we all remain as onlookers? We are likely to end up with laws that automatically remove the family from an incapacitated person's life decisions and actions, under the theory that the state always knows better than the family. And perhaps this situation might allow a person who has never made unwise or unsafe decisions before dementia set in to be in jeopardy as a result.

When Can the Media Really Help?

I've gotten calls from people who felt abandoned after their story was published or broadcast. The journalist who interviewed them, they told themselves, would make all their troubles disappear. This is magical thinking. If you are the person who is aggrieved, then *you* are the one who must act.

Amicus briefs can help. That's part of the story of how my gag order was lifted. The *Albuquerque Journal* added its voice in support of lifting the gag order to my own already-filed plea asking for the gag order to be lifted.

In that situation, however, I didn't ask the *Journal* to help me. The newspaper decided on their own to do that. But my attorney had already petitioned the court for this relief many months before the *Journal* was even aware that a gag order existed.

Had the judge in District Court not lifted my gag order at that point, at least one large, national organization had told me it was willing to file an amicus brief in federal court to support my arguments. (Even while under a gag order, my attorney and I were legally able to speak to other attorneys together.)

Finally, let's say you had a gag order but managed to get it lifted. Now, there can only be lasting repercussions for you if you deliberately say something that's untrue about the former guardian, conservator, or trustee. You're free!

If you decide to vent, make sure you have all the documents we've been discussing all along and that they're in order and support your statements before contacting any members of the media. Over the years, I knew people who tried to contact Oprah Winfrey and Montell Williams, but they had no documentation. They didn't even get a callback.[106]

Getting gag orders lifted after the death of the ward is a whole other matter. A preliminary national reform might be for the states to change their laws so that gag orders expire automatically when a person who was under guardianship is no longer alive. I believe that they should all expire when the ward dies.

What could possibly be so worth hiding that the public can't ever be told, and even if the heirs know what happened, they must be kept from speaking? Classified material containing government secrets is usually released after fifty years. Should these family documents be considered even "more sensitive" than matters of national security?

As an aside, once everyone sees the documents, it might become clear that—if your loved one was assigned a dishonest guardian—you've all been lied to throughout the guardianship. About your loved one, about the situation, and even about each other. You might find yourself becoming better able to deal with those family members you thought were against you. You have likely all been maligned and manipulated. You might discover that you have more in common than you thought you did.

Isn't it ironic that uniting in wanting your freedom back might be the only motivation capable of bringing family members who were alienated from each other years earlier back together? You might all realize that the lies you heard were cruel and deliberate strategies to drive your family apart. Now, that would be a proper punishment for an unscrupulous guardian who made any existing family disagreements much worse when the case was in progress, wouldn't it?

The local or district court will look foolish trying to enforce an unconstitutional gag order. You might be able to find nonprofits willing to help you with amicus briefs.

Individuals don't seem to have much luck setting up their own commercial-guardianship-bashing websites. Of the two sites I was keeping track of that were truly public and allowed aggrieved family members a direct voice, those are both gone.

The only remaining ones are administered by nonprofits—primarily the National Association to Stop Guardianship Abuse[107] and the Center for Estate Administration Reform.[108] A third site, Guardianabusecases.org, once existed solely to gather stories of abuse by commercial guardians. However, almost everything on the third site was posted anonymously or under a pseudonym. It has now vanished, and the Wayback Machine has no record that it ever existed.[109]

There's a similar site in Australia—the Australian Association to STOP Guardianship and Administration Abuse.[110] Sometimes, they can help with advice.

Complaint systems exist everywhere, attesting to the fact that the problem is worldwide. Considering the increasing numbers of complaints, what we're doing in this area doesn't seem to be working too well.

Can Changing Your Own Situation Ultimately Solve the Problem?

The current situation won't change overnight. Wishing for this to happen won't make it so, nor will a small number of active citizens lobbying their legislators. We need a large, well-organized group taking action to change the situation. Several small nonprofits discovered this after they tried the lobbying route for a decade or more. Despite a few hard-won successes in individual cases, they've ultimately found meaningful reform elusive.

Given how coercive and painful our system is for the families involved, perhaps the opinion I'm about to offer might seem counterintuitive. I suspect the most efficient way to create change in the system is first to change yourself. You have total control over how you respond to the situation. (I can hear Jack Canfield's voice reverberating in my memory as I say this. It's one of the lessons he teaches repeatedly.) And no, this is not a Pollyanna approach.

Three major issues seem to underlie all the other problems:

The first is that most adult children know nothing about the issue of dependent adults until they're faced with a loved one in need. I hope this book has now allowed readers to prepare for many of the aspects of that eventuality.

The second issue is the lack of timely access to good legal help. If you can't keep a lawyer on retainer at the cost of $1,000 or more per month, you can certainly subscribe to a service like LegalShield that keeps one on call 24/7. That way, you don't have to guess what the law permits you to do and what legal documents mean. You can also get an attorney's letter written easily and cheaply, or even free, as part of your subscription, if you need one.

The final problem is not enough money. It doesn't matter whether that money is for medical expenses or to pursue justice. If you don't have it, you can't spend it. Adult children who are less affluent than their parents also tend to perpetuate the stereotype of idle sons and daughters who while away their time partying on a tropical beach as they rack up debts that make them hungry for their inheritance.

A related problem that flows from dealing with legal issues is the amount of time it often takes for a court case to inch, snail-like, through the legal system, but we won't be able to fix that here.

Absolute dependence on a single job or employer is highly unlikely ever to give you financial freedom. If you're barely making expenses, regardless of what those are, you won't be able to absorb any financial blow, let alone an expensive ongoing elder care or legal situation.

Here's how the financial drama plays out for most people: they have jobs or, if they're entrepreneurs, they seem to be working constantly to keep their businesses viable. If they have domestic partners with jobs or who also own businesses, then both people are dependent on the solvency of their employer or business. Will an employee (even at the highest levels of corporate management) be needed next week? Will that small business stay afloat?

Getting all your income from only one source is financially danger-ous, even if you're not immediately faced with caring for an additional dependent. Nor will investments that create no income for you but are designed to grow in value over a long period help your cash flow, unless you sell them. Depending on the tax laws at that moment, you might lose a large portion of that money to taxes.

So many businesses closed during COVID-19 and never reopened! Others reopened but never fully recovered and eventually shuttered their doors. The Bureau of Labor Statistics tells us that 14.6 million people lost their private sector jobs in 2020.[111] Employers large and small have announced layoffs over the past few years, including such corporate giants as Amazon, Meta, and Google.[112]

Today, you can't afford to believe that you'll hold your current job until you retire, even if your employer is a major corporation. Now all of us need other sources of income as insurance against insolvency; other income streams, if you will. I alluded to this problem earlier when I suggested that those who plan to become family caregivers need to create some source of passive or at least residual income so they don't have to leave an incapacitated loved one alone because they must leave their home to make a living.

However, any business that succeeds must fill a genuine need. With the advent of AI, it has become ever easier to do the necessary market research, find a preferred audience, and begin work.

Just a final reminder of the real-world situation: *Newsweek* reported in August 2024 that in addition to their full-time jobs, many Gen Xers are spending an additional thirty-seven hours weekly caring for aging loved ones. About three-quarters of them say they can't save for retirement. And a full 63 percent say they're living from one paycheck to the next so they can care for aging parents.[113] The Baby Boomers have been down this road before them. Two generations, financially cannibalized by the eldercare spider and its web. Isn't it time we broke free?

You want to care for your parents and your children, but you don't want to become financially strapped in this process. And you certainly want to prevent your loved ones from falling into the web of the commercial guardianship system. So, you must find methods of earning income that won't require you to trade your time away from home for a per-hour wage from an employer.

What I'm proposing is a variation on a concept Warren Buffet told us all years ago. He said, "If you don't learn to make money while you sleep, you will work until you die."[114]

What I'm suggesting is that, if you don't have passive income streams, you won't have enough money to carry you through a time when you're caring for both growing children and aging parents. Do I know how long that period is likely to be? No. And neither do you. And, if you have to be home supervising someone with dementia, you can't be away from home taking extra jobs, even if you have forty-eight hours in a day.

I know of one person who found that operating vending machines paid her bills for quite some time. The effort to maintain them and collect the money people inserted into them required perhaps a couple of hours per week. But if she'd had to stay home to supervise an incapacitated person, this alternative wouldn't have been an ideal situation for her.

It takes some initial effort to set up an online business, but with good preparation, it can be done. If successful, after a few years it will offer you some real independence and the ability to pay for what you and your loved ones need. The time to start is as soon as you can, so that you won't need hours and hours to do this while you're also being faced with becoming a caregiver.

While attending Canadian serial entrepreneur Tom Matzen's workshop on passive and residual income, I realized that I had followed a different course from the beginning, always building revenue streams. These came from book royalties, writing, dividends, publicly traded REITs, publicly traded limited partnerships, and bonds. Years ago, when banks were paying higher interest rates, I also owned CDs.

Investing isn't rocket science. If I could do this, so can you. My passive income strategy gave me the financial protection that allowed me to survive fourteen years of slogging through the legal guardianship swamp. When I needed to spend several years working on documents relating to my mother's case, I could afford to 'retire' to do that. I didn't have to trade my time for an hourly wage. This method allowed me to emerge from that lengthy ordeal still solvent and ultimately also freed from the spider's web of restrictions placed on me by a court-imposed gag order.

But now, the financial scene has changed. The formerly 'good' 5 percent to 7 percent returns of most standard passive or residual investments might not cover inflation. A look at how prices in the grocery store have risen over the past few years should be all you'll need to convince you of this.

During the years when I engaged in increasing amounts of defensive investing, I never thought of it as financial insurance in case I later had unexpected dependents. But that's exactly what it turned out to be. As a result of my experience, and as I compare what happened in my case to other people I have known, I've come to realize that we all need this sort of protection.

Higher up on the scale of solvency-protectors are other less-traditional investments—at least less traditional for middle-class people—that are not stocks or bonds. They're other passive and residual income producers that exceed 7 percent of your annual income. These include profitable businesses, sometimes where your only action is buying into the enterprise. Someone else is managing them, but you get paid, at stated intervals, out of their cash flow.

Other possibilities include creating an internet service that can almost run on autopilot. There are also investment groups (syndicates) that specialize in buying and leasing buildings that combine residential and commercial tenants (again run by a manager, not you). Some renovate properties they don't own, leasing them from the owner, and then leasing them for more money to a third party (once more, someone else does the work; you don't). Then come various sorts of angel investing (obtaining a stake in a viable business or revenue from an existing business), and private lending. All of these offer a potentially better rate of return than most stocks and bonds.

No one can predict the outcome of a lawsuit, and no one can promise you that you'll get rich from any or even all these investments. You need to be part of a good team. Vet your colleagues, as well as each individual deal, carefully. However, what I can promise you about money sitting in a bank is this: it's losing buying power to inflation every year. You need $18,208.36 in 2024 to buy what $10,000 would have bought you back in 2000. You stand a much better chance of improving your life if you take carefully considered action, rather than letting outside forces manipulate you.

Thank you for allowing me to act as your guide on your journey toward understanding where we are now and envisioning how you'd like the system to improve. At least you've realized what's happening out there and where you and your family might fit into the picture. I hope that all of you who've seen flaws in this system will continue to work—and to unite with others—to improve the situation. Please let me know what you've been doing and whether there are other things you think I can do to help.

Conclusion

I've just taken you on a trip down the quicksand-filled trail that those touched by our extremely flawed adult guardianship system must walk. You're now acquainted with its obstacles and have figured out how to overcome many of them.

Your biggest challenge will likely be allowing yourself to believe in your own capacity to survive. One major stumbling block will be your own inertia. It's hard to let go of the belief that someone else must change something outside of you before the system can change.

Just imagine being in a situation where you must take responsibility for one or more elders, but you yourself are financially free. You don't have to worry about whether you'll have enough money to care for a loved one or pay for an attorney and still take care of your family! Then your only concern can be what's best for you and those you love. Isn't that the way things should be?

TAKEAWAYS

1. Understand, as completely as you can, what you want to accomplish and why.
2. Research what the form of action you choose will require in terms of time, energy, and money before proceeding.
3. Allow yourself to believe in your own ability to cope with changing circumstances.
4. Now, you can be financially free to make whatever decisions are best for you and your loved ones.

Notes

1   Léonie Rosenstiel. *Protecting Mama: Surviving the Legal Guardianship Swamp.* (2nd edition) Minneapolis, MN: Calumet Editions, NM, 2023

2   Léonie Rosenstiel. *Legal Protection: Affordable Options for Individuals, Families, and Small Businesses.* Albuquerque, NM: Dayspring Resources, Inc., 2024.

3   See: https://law.justia.com/cases/pennsylvania/superior-court/2012/536-eda-2011.html (Accessed May 15, 2024)

4   "Filial Responsibility Laws by State 2024" at: https://worldpopulationreview.com/state-rankings/filial-responsibility-laws-by-state (Accessed May 15, 2024)

5   See: https://law.justia.com/cases/north-dakota/supreme-court/2013/20120432.html

6   See: https://law.justia.com/cases/pennsylvania/superior-court/2015/1342-wda-2014.html

7   Joyce Famakinwa, "Health Care Bankruptcies Are Skyrocketing, But Not Yet in Home Health," July 28, 2023, https://homehealthcarenews.com/2023/07/health-care-bankruptcies-are-skyrocketing-but-not-yet-in-home-based-care/ (Accessed September 17, 2024.)

8   Dietrich Knauth, "US nursing home operator LaVie files for bankruptcy to downsize, shed debts," June 3, 2024, Reuters (Accessed September 17, 2024.)

9   Joyce Famakinwa, *ibid.*

10 For the full story, see: Léonie Rosenstiel, *Protecting Mama: Surviving the Legal Guardianship Swamp.*

11 This is part of a system called "The Success Principles," taught by self-development guru Jack Canfield. See: Jack Canfield, "The Success Formula that Puts You in Control of Your Destiny," https://jackcanfield.com/blog/the-formula-that-puts-you-in-control-of-success/ (Accessed May 26, 2024)

12 https://www.nami.org/about-mental-illness/mental-health-by-the-numbers/#:~:text=22.8%25%20of%20U.S.%20adults%20experienced,represents%201%20in%2020%20adults. (Accessed May 25, 2024)

13 https://www.pewresearch.org/short-reads/2023/07/24/8-facts-about-americans-with-disabilities/#:~:text=Overall%2C%20there%20are%20about%2042.5,care%20or%20independent%20living%20difficulties. (Accessed May 25, 2024)

14 https://www.alz.org/alzheimers-dementia/facts-figures#:~:text=in%20each%20state-,Quick%20facts,65%20and%20older%20in%202021. (Accessed May 25, 2024)

15 https://finance.yahoo.com/news/3-reasons-why-boomers-eating-103700045. html#:~:text=Baby%20boomers%20have%20an%20average,Mutual's%20 Planning%20%26%20Progress%20Study%202024. (Accessed May 25, 2024)

16 https://news.northwesternmutual.com/planning-and-progress-2019 (Accessed May 26, 2024).

17 Maurie Blackman, "3 reasons why baby boomers are eating through their retirement savings so quickly," https://finance.yahoo.com/news/3-reasons-why-boomers-eating-103700045.html#:~:text=Baby%20boomers%20 have%20an%20average,Mutual's%20Planning%20%26%20Progress%20 Study%202024. (Accessed September 7, 2024)

18 http://amygoyer.com/joomla/index.php/about-amy

19 https://finance.yahoo.com/news/3-reasons-why-boomers-eating-103700045. html#:~:text=Baby%20boomers%20have%20an%20average,Mutual's%20 Planning%20%26%20Progress%20Study%202024.

20 Finance of America acquired AAG in December 2022. See: https://www. nationalmortgagenews.com/news/finance-of-america-acquiring-top-reverse-lender-aag More information about how this situation is going to cause problems for society in the future can be found in the financial section of the Dayspring Empowerment Course and Summit.

21 This topic is also covered in depth, in my Dayspring Empowerment Summit and my Dayspring Empowerment Course.

22 https://realestate.usnews.com/real-estate/articles/how-i-budget-to-live-in-the-most-expensive-city-in-the-us (Accessed May 26, 2024)

23 In my Empowerment Course, I offer more detailed tools for calculating expenses and comparing how much providing for specific services and needs costs in different cities.

24 My mother, who died just before her 101st birthday, would have been broke for almost seventeen years, if she had used this method for her entire retirement.

25 https://finance.yahoo.com/news/many-americans-retire-million-dol-lars-140019814.html#:~:text=However%2C%20not%20a%20huge%20 percentage,million%20or%20more%20in%20savings. (Accessed on May 26, 2024)

26 For more on how to overcome physical hazards, listen to Linda MacDougall's presentation in my Dayspring Empowerment Summit or consult Modules 1 and 2 of the Dayspring Empowerment Course.

27 https://myelder.com/are-so-called-free-elder-care-referral-agencies-really-free/#:~:text=Adult%20care%20homes%20and%20nursing,pay%20the%20 best%20commission%20fees (Accessed September 7, 2024.).

28 "Continuing Care Communities FAQs." Pennsylvania Insurance Department from: https://www.insurance.pa.gov/Coverage/ContinuingCare/Pages/Con-tinuingCareRetirementCommunitiesFAQs.aspx (Accessed September 7, 2024.)

29 https://www.leadinghomecare.com/paying-for-referrals/

30   He discusses this idea in more detail during my Empowerment Summit.
31   How and why to evaluate these needs and desires is detailed in the Dayspring Empowerment Course, and to a lesser extent in the Dayspring Empowerment Summit.
32   "Parens Patriae," Legal Information Institute, Cornell Law School. https://www.law.cornell.edu/wex/parens_patriae (Accessed September 17, 2024.)
33   "A Pattern Recognition Theory of Mind," April 28, 2018; revised January 20, 2022. https://fortelabs.com/blog/a-pattern-recognition-theory-of-mind/ (Accessed September 17, 2024.)
34   Adolf Berger, Barry Nicholas, and Susan M. Tregiari, "guardianship, Roman," *Oxford Classical Dictionary*, https://doi.org/10.1093/acrefore/9780199381135.013.7229 (Accessed September 7, 2024.
35   https://www.nia.nih.gov/health/alzheimers-symptoms-and-diagnosis/what-are-signs-alzheimers-disease#:~:text=As%20the%20disease%20progresses%2C%20symptoms,their%20mid%2D60s%20or%20later. (Accessed May 26, 2024)
36   Corrie Pelc, "Alzheimer's study controversy: Where do we go from here?" August 2, 2022. https://www.medicalnewstoday.com/articles/alzheimers-study-controversy-what-does-it-mean-for-future-research (Accessed September 17, 2024.)
37   For more detailed discussion of this issue, listen to my online Dayspring Empowerment Course and Linda MacDougall's presentation in the Dayspring Empowerment Summit.
38   See: https://www.usaging.org/Files/Workforce-Issues_508.pdf (Accessed May 26, 2024)
39   "Caregiver Burnout," https://my.clevelandclinic.org/health/diseases/9225-caregiver-burnout (Accessed November 23, 2024)
40   "Three Individuals Arrested and Charged for Neglect Resulting in Death," NM DOJ. See: https://nmdoj.gov/press-release/three-individuals-arrested-and-charged-for-neglect-resulting-in-death-of-a-woman-with-autism/#:~:text=%E2%80%9CThe%20abuse%20and%20neglect%20that,no%20other%20word%20for%20it.%E2%80%9D (Accessed September 7, 2024)
41   Module 6 of the Dayspring Empowerment Course and the video by Alexandra Snyder in the Dayspring Empowerment Summit have more information.
42   https://www.annuityexpertadvice.com/paying-healthcare-long-term-care-costs/ (Accessed May 27, 2024)
43   https://www.census.gov/library/stories/2021/04/who-had-medical-debt-in-united-states.html (Accessed May 27, 2024)
44   I treat this issue in more detail in the Dayspring Empowerment Course and in other contexts.
45   https://worldwidebusinessbrokers.com/how-many-businesses-sell/. Accessed July 17, 2024,

46   https://www.cnn.com/interactive/2024/10/politics/political-fundraising-elderly-election-invs-dg/ Accessed December 1, 2024

47   https://www.prudential.com/financial-education/4-percent-rule-retirement#:~:text=If%20you%20have%20limited%20savings,spend%20on%20the%20same%20items. (Accessed May 27, 2024)

48   https://taxfoundation.org/data/all/state/2023-state-tax-data/ (Accessed May 26, 2024). Comparative statistics available on that page now go back to the 2009 report.

49   https://www.debt.org/credit/cards/how-to-lower-interest-rate/

50   https://unitedfcu.com/you/financial-calculators/credit-calculators/how-long-until-i-pay-off-loan (Accessed May 27, 2024)

51   https://data.bls.gov/cgi-bin/cpicalc.pl?cost1=90%2C000andyear1=200311andyear2=202407 (Accessed May 27, 2024)

52   For more detail, see the Dayspring Empowerment Course and listen to the Dayspring Empowerment Summit presentation by Erik Gallegos, a securities broker with an insurance license who also has a master's degree in international finance.

53   Ibidem

54   For more on this subject, consult Topic 7 of "Common Questions and Considerations" at: https://dayspringresources.com/faq/ and https://dayspringresources.com/probate-terms-of-art/ (Accessed May 27, 2024). More detailed information on the issues involved in billing during a commercial guardianship/conservatorship is in *Protecting Mama*, in the Dayspring Empowerment Summit and in the Dayspring Empowerment Course.

55   For more detail consult *Protecting Mama*, the Dayspring Empowerment Summit, the Dayspring Empowerment Course and the Knowledgebase.

56   "Bankruptcy of insurance and reinsurance companies in the United States," *Atlas Magazine*, January 2019, https://www.atlas-mag.net/en/article/bankruptcy-of-insurance-and-reinsurance-companies-in-the-usa (Accessed September 16, 2024)

57   For more detail on these matters, consult the course resources, the summit, and the Dayspring website.

58   I go into detail, in my book *Protecting Mama*, about how powers of attorney were used to manipulate Mama and me just before and during her competency hearing.

59   https://www.youtube.com/watch?v=h3QSq8I9_IM (Accessed May 27, 2024)

60   Robert Frank, "Do the Rockefellers Still Matter?" *Wall Street Journal*, May 27, 2008. https://www.wsj.com/articles/BL-WHB-383 (Accessed May 27, 2024).

61   I detail the disagreements in my own family and their seismic emotional effects in the Dayspring Empowerment Course, and in *Protecting Mama*, as well as in its forthcoming prequels.

62   There's an extensive discussion of this issue in *Protecting Mama*, on the Dayspring website, and as part of the Dayspring Empowerment Summit and the Dayspring Empowerment Course.

63   The whole idea of who gets the guardianship or conservatorship, and why, and how, is treated more fully in *Protecting Mama*, and in the Dayspring Empowerment Course and the Dayspring Empowerment summit.

64   As quoted in Newsweek, February 20, 1978. Cited in AZ Quotes. https://www.azquotes.com/quote/76554 (Accessed September 8, 2024.)

65   John Leland, "I'm Petitioning…for the Return of My Life," New York Times, December 7, 2018, https://www.nytimes.com/2018/12/07/nyregion/court-appointed-guardianship-like-prison.html (Accessed September 17 2024; other sources report that the judge had an only slightly less gruesome demise.)

66   I'm not aware of any states in which the contracted LegalShield law firm has such ethical conflicts.

67   "What Percentage of Lawsuits Settle before Trial?…" The Law Dictionary. https://thelawdictionary.org/article/what-percentage-of-lawsuits-settle-before-trial-what-are-some-statistics-on-personal-injury-settlements/#:~:text=According%20to%20the%20most%20recently,by%20a%20judge%20or%20jury. (Accessed September 17, 2024.)

68   https://lifelegal.org/about/endorsements/

69   For more on the mechanics of how this sort of law has been used unjustly, consult my course and summit, and my blogs.

70   https://milkeninstitute.org/centers/center-for-the-future-of-aging (Accessed May 27, 2024

71   Ric Edelman, "The Ric Edelman Show," KKOB-AM, Albuquerque, NM. Aired December 5, 2020.

72   Additional information on this is on the Dayspring website, and in Dayspring educational products.

73   For more information, see: https://rosenstielleonie2.wearelegalshield.com/ This affiliate website explains what the firm can do for people. Remember to select your state or Canadian province from the menu in the upper left-hand corner.

74   https://amzn.to/3TAOIED

75   Yamri Taddese, "Ombudsman cites 'recurring concerns' with Office of Public Guardian and Trustee," *Canadian Lawyer*, July 30, 2015, https://www.canadianlawyermag.com/news/general/ombudsman-cites-recurring-concerns-with-office-of-public-guardian-and-trustee/273321 (Accessed September 17, 2024)

76   https://aasgaa.org/ (Accessed September 17, 2024.)

77   Chuck Norris, "To Restore Spirit and Health, the Best Move You Can Make Is Outdoors," May 8, 2015, https://www.creators.com/read/c-force/05/15/to-restore-spirit-and-health-the-best-move-you-can-make-is-outdoors (Accessed September 17, 2024.)

78   Jennifer Braster, "You Receive a Subpoena For [sic.] a Client's File—What Do You Do?" Las Vegas, NV: Naylor and Braster, June 3, 2022. https://www.naylorandbrasterlaw.com/

you-receive-a-subpoena-for-a-clients-file-what-do-you-do/ (Accessed September 17, 2024.)

79   They were readily accessible when I began my research, but, as of May 27, 2024, were secured behind a pay wall.

80   I've treated other specific different breathing exercises in the Dayspring Empowerment Course.

81   A useful interactive web page on paid family caregiving is: https://www.joingivers.com/how-to-get-paid-take-care-of-family#states

82   "Cost of Care Survey," https://www.genworth.com/aging-and-you/finances/cost-of-care (Accessed September 6, 2024)

83   Thomas Carlyle (transl.), *Wilhelm Meister's Apprenticeship and Travels*, Vol. I (of 2), p. 393 The Project Gutenberg eBook of Wilhelm Meister's Apprenticeship and Travels, Vol. I (of 2) (Accessed November 22, 2024)

84   https://www.woundedwarriorproject.org/programs/benefits-services (Accessed June 1, 2024). After coping with a serious overspending scandal in 2016, by 2019 the nonprofit had named new leadership and regained its reputation.

85   https://www.caregiveraction.org/agencies-and-organizations/ (Accessed September 17, 2024.)

86   https://www.guardianship.org/wp-content/uploads/NGA-Standards-2022.pdf (Accessed September 17, 2024.)

87   https://www.nmhealth.org/publication/view/form/8602/ (Accessed June 1, 2024)

88   The English version is at: https://ww2.nycourts.gov/sites/default/files/document/files/2017-11/ENGLISH.pdf (Accessed September 6, 2024)

89   "Elder Care Locator," https://eldercare.acl.gov/Public/Index.aspx (Accessed September 6, 2024)

90   I show you a process of narrowing down your best choices of people to consult and courses of action the Dayspring Empowerment Course.(Accessed September 6, 2024)

91   "Grant information," https://alzfdn.org/find-a-member/grant-information/ (Accessed September 9, 2024)

92   The Dayspring Empowerment Course discusses how to evaluate your options.

93   https://slate.com/human-interest/2014/11/sol-wachtler-the-judge-who-coined-indict-a-ham-sandwich-was-himself-indicted.html (Accessed May 28, 2024).

94   She is interviewed as part of the Dayspring Empowerment Summit.

95   A subject discussed further in *Protecting Mama*.

96   William Blackstone, *Commentaries on the Law (Book the Fourth)*, Lonang Institute: Livonia, MI, 2005, p. 208 (originally published in 1769). (Accessed September 9, 2024)

97   "Dispute Resolution Quotes," https://www.adrtoolbox.com/library/adr-quotes/. (Accessed September 9, 2024.)

98 "Top 50 Melvin Belli Quotes and Sayings," https://www.inspiringquotes.us/author/4953-melvin-belli (Accessed September 9, 2024.)

99 In *Protecting Mama*, and in the Dayspring Empowerment Course, you can find more detail on these subjects.

100 Sibyl Nicholson, "AI Proves to be 10% Faster and More Accurate than Top Human Attorneys," https://interestingengineering.com/innovation/ai-proves-to-be-10-faster-and-more-accurate-than-top-human-lawyers (Accessed September 9, 2024. This article originally appeared in 2018. AI has become far faster and more accurate since then.)

101 See: (PDF) Guardianship reform arrives in Canada A court-ordered legislative reform in Nova Scotia has made historic gains for adults with intellectual disabilities (researchgate.net). This is a free download. (Accessed September 17, 2024.)

102 https://novascotia.ca/just/pto/adult-capacity-decision.asp#:~:text=The%20Adult%20Capacity%20and%20Decision%2Dmaking%20Act%20is%20for%20people,be%20shown%20that%20they%20cannot (Accessed September 9, 2024)

103 https://www.washingtonpost.com/nation/2023/11/04/florida-guardian-ship-investigation-safeguards/ (Accessed June 9, 2024)

104 https://dictionary.cambridge.org/us/dictionary/english/publish (Accessed18 May 28, 2024)

105 https://www.abcactionnews.com/news/local-news/i-team-investigates/the-price-of-protection/price-of-protection-woman-loses-seffner-home-after-fathers-guardian-sues-her-for-libel (Accessed June 3, 2024).

106 For more detail, consult the Dayspring Empowerment Summit and the Dayspring Empowerment Course.

107 https://stopguardianabuse.org/ (Accessed September 17, 2024.)

108 https://www.cearjustice.org/ (Accessed September 17, 2024.)

109 https://web.archive.org/web/*/http://guardianshipabusecases.org/* (Accessed September 17, 2024.)

110 https://aasgaa.org/ (Accessed September 17, 2024.)

111 "Unemployment rises in 2020, as the country battles the COVID-19 pandemic," June 2021, https://www.bls.gov/opub/mlr/2021/article/unem-ployment-rises-in-2020-as-the-country-battles-the-covid-19-pandemic.htm (Accessed June 15, 2024.)

112 https://www.statista.com/statistics/1127080/worldwide-tech-layoffs-covid-19-biggest/ (Accessed May 28, 2024.)

113 "Gen X Caring For [Sic.] Parents, Kids Living 'Paycheck-to-Paycheck' Study Shows," August 13-14, 2024, Newsweek Magazine. https://www.newsweek.com/gen-x-caring-parents-study-shows-1938686 (Accessed September 17, 2024.)

114 Will Healy, "The 8-Step Plan To Achieving Financial Freedom," July 12, 2021. https://finance.yahoo.com/news/8-step-plan-achieving-financial-210034255.html (Accessed September 17, 2024.)

About the Author

Born in New York City, Léonie Rosenstiel has traveled to four continents (if you count Central America). She admits to having spent "a lot of time" in school, earning degrees in fields as diverse as musicology, public health, ministry, and East Asian medicine. Her life journey has also brought her into frequent contact with attorneys, social workers, and healthcare professionals, in large part because she spent long periods as a caregiver for her husband and her mother—nine years each.

Léonie regularly teaches and speaks to groups, and she coaches and consults with individuals and families. She has interviewed attorneys, judges, 'professional' guardians, and caregivers to discover both the problems and the possible solutions to the difficulties people have when confronting family issues.

Her Amazon bestselling book *Protecting Mama: Surviving the Legal Guardianship Swarm,* has won more than fifty literary awards. As of this writing, her book *Legal Protection: Affordable Options for Individuals, Families, and Small Businesses* has been on the Amazon bestseller list in its category since January 5, 2024, and has won another four. She also created the *Dayspring Empowerment Summit* and the *Dayspring Empowerment Course.* She is a frequent panelist and a popular podcast guest. To contact her, email: leonie@dayspringresources.com. Visit her website at https://DayspringResources.com.

Have you had family experience of these problems? You might be eligible to become a mentor of others, using the Dayspring® Empowerment System. In that case, put "Mentor" in the subject line of your email to Léonie.

If, instead, you think you'd like to write about your experience, write to Léonie and put "Anthology Guidelines" in the subject line of your email.

Léonie now lives in Albuquerque, New Mexico, where she loves to nurse a cup of Earl Grey tea while watching the sunrise over the Sandia Mountains.

Check out the author's other activities and publications:

Protecting Mama: Surviving the Legal Guardianship Swamp (Calumet Editions)

Legal Protection: Affordable Options for Individuals, Families, and Small Businesses (Dayspring Resources)

Nadia Boulanger: A Life in Music (W. W. Norton)

Website: https://dayspringresources.com

Contact email: leonie@dayspingresources.com

Dayspring Resources, Inc. offers techniques and helps to empower the families of elders.

Léonie Rosenstiel is available for interviews and frequently speaks to online groups. Contact her at the email above for more information. Please let her know whether there are other subjects you'd like her to research.